MICROSOFT AZURE EXAM DP-201: DESIGNING AN AZURE DATA SOLUTION PRACTICE QUESTIONS & DUMPS WITH EXPLANATIONS

70+ EXAM PRACTICE QUESTIONS FOR DP-201: MICROSOFT AZURE EXAM UPDATED 2020

Presented By: Vortex Books

VORTEX

Books

About Vortex Books:

Vortex Books is a publishing company based in San Francisco, California, USA, a platform that is available both online & locally, which unleashes the power of technical and educational content. Our aim is to provide help to individuals who are eager to learn and excel in technical certifications and other educational fields. Vortex Books was founded in 2017, and is now distributing books globally.

Testlet 1 Case study

This is a case study. Case studies are not timed separately. You can use as much exam time as you would like to complete each case. However, there may be additional case studies and sections on this exam. You must manage your time to ensure that you are able to complete all questions included on this exam in the time provided.

To answer the questions included in a case study, you will need to reference information that is provided in the case study. Case studies might contain exhibits and other resources that provide more information about the scenario that is described in the case study. Each question is independent of the other questions in this case study.

At the end of this case study, a review screen will appear. This screen allows you to review your answers and to make changes before you move to the next section of the exam. After you begin a new section, you cannot return to this section.

To start the case study
To display the first question in this case study, click the **Next** button. Use the buttons in the left pane to explore the content of the case study before you answer the questions. Clicking these buttons displays information such as business requirements, existing environment, and problem statements. If the case study has an **All Information** tab, note that the information displayed is identical to the information displayed on the subsequent tabs. When you are ready to answer a question, click the **Question** button to return to the question.

Background

Trey Research is a technology innovator. The company partners with regional transportation department office to build solutions that improve traffic flow and safety. The company is developing the following solutions:

Solution	Comments
Real Time Response	This solution will detect sudden changes in traffic flow including slow downs and stops that persist for more than one minute. The system will automatically dispatch emergency response vehicles to investigate issues. The solution will use a PySpark script to detect traffic flow changes. Script performance will be limited by available memory.
Backtrack	This solution will allow public safety officials to locate vehicles on roadways that implement traffic sensors. The solution must report changes in real time.
Planning Assistance	Transportation organizations will use Planning Assistance to analyze traffic data. The solution will allow users to define reports based on queries of the traffic data. The reports can be used for the following analyses: • current traffic load • correlation with recent local events susch as sporting events • historical traffic • tracking the travel of a single vehicle

Regional transportation departments installed traffic sensor systems on major highways across North America. Sensors record the following information each time a vehicle passes in front of a sensor:

- Time
- Location in latitude and longitude Speed in kilometers per second (kmps) License plate number
- Length of vehicle in meters
- Sensors provide data by using the following structure:

```
{
    "time" : "2014-09-15T23:14:25.72511732",
    "location" : {
      "type": "Point",
      "coordinates": [
            31.9.
            -4.8
      ]
    },
    "speed": 66.2,
    "license_plate": "WA-AJ0072W",
    "vehicle_length": 4.5
}
```

Traffic sensors will occasionally capture an image of a vehicle for debugging purposes. You must optimize performance of saving/storing vehicle images.

Traffic sensor data
- Sensors must have permission only to add items to the SensorData collection. Traffic data insertion rate must be maximized.
- Once every three months all traffic sensor data must be analyzed to look for data patterns that indicate sensor malfunctions. Sensor data must be stored in a Cosmos DB named treydata in a collection named SensorData
- The impact of vehicle images on sensor data throughout must be minimized.

Backtrack

This solution reports on all data related to a specific vehicle license plate. The report must use data from the SensorData collection. Users must be able to filter vehicle data in the following ways:

- vehicles on a specific road
- vehicles driving above the speed limit

Planning Assistance

Data used for Planning Assistance must be stored in a sharded Azure SQL Database.

Data from the Sensor Data collection will automatically be loaded into the Planning Assistance database once a week by using Azure Data Factory. You must be able to manually trigger the data load process.

Privacy and security policy

- Azure Active Directory must be used for all services where it is available.
- For privacy reasons, license plate number information must not be accessible in Planning Assistance.
- Unauthorized usage of the Planning Assistance data must be detected as quickly as possible. Unauthorized usage is determined by looking for an unusual pattern of usage.
- Data must only be stored for seven years.

Performance and availability

- The report for Backtrack must execute as quickly as possible.
- The SLA for Planning Assistance is 70 percent, and multiday outages are permitted. All data must be replicated to multiple geographic regions to prevent data loss.
- You must maximize the performance of the Real Time Response system.

Financial requirements

Azure resource costs must be minimized where possible.

QUESTION 1
You need to design the vehicle images storage solution.
What should you recommend?

A. Azure Media Services
B. Azure Premium Storage account
C. Azure Redis Cache
D. Azure Cosmos DB

Correct Answer: B

Explanation/Reference:
Explanation:
Premium Storage stores data on the latest technology Solid
State Drives (SSDs) whereas Standard Storage stores data on
Hard Disk Drives (HDDs). Premium Storage is designed for
Azure Virtual Machine workloads which require consistent high
IO performance and low latency in order to host IO intensive
workloads like OLTP, Big Data, and Data Warehousing on
platforms like SQL Server, MongoDB, Cassandra, and others.
With Premium Storage, more customers will be able to lift-and-
shift demanding enterprise applications to the cloud.

Scenario: Traffic sensors will occasionally capture an image of
a vehicle for debugging purposes. You must optimize
performance of saving/storing vehicle images.
The impact of vehicle images on sensor data throughout must
be minimized.

Reference:
https://azure.microsoft.com/es-es/blog/introducing-premium-
storage-high-performance-storage-for-azure-virtual-machine-
workloads/

QUESTION 2

You need to design a sharding strategy for the Planning Assistance database. What should you recommend?

A. a list mapping shard map on the binary representation of the License Plate column
B. a range mapping shard map on the binary representation of the speed column
C. a list mapping shard map on the location column
D. a range mapping shard map on the time column

Correct Answer: A

Explanation/Reference:
Explanation:
Data used for Planning Assistance must be stored in a sharded Azure SQL Database.

A shard typically contains items that fall within a specified range determined by one or more attributes of the data. These attributes form the shard key (sometimes referred to as the partition key). The shard key should be static. It shouldn't be based on data that might change.

Reference:
https://docs.microsoft.com/en-us/azure/architecture/patterns/sharding

QUESTION 3

You need to recommend an Azure SQL Database pricing tier for Planning Assistance. Which pricing tier should you recommend?

A. Business critical Azure SQL Database single database
B. General purpose Azure SQL Database Managed Instance
C. Business critical Azure SQL Database Managed Instance
D. General purpose Azure SQL Database single database

Correct Answer: B

Explanation/Reference:
Explanation:
Azure resource costs must be minimized where possible.
Data used for Planning Assistance must be stored in a sharded Azure SQL Database. The SLA for Planning Assistance is 70 percent, and multiday outages are permitted.

Testlet 2 Case study

This is a case study. Case studies are not timed separately. You can use as much exam time as you would like to complete each case. However, there may be additional case studies and sections on this exam. You must manage your time to ensure that you are able to complete all questions included on this exam in the time provided.

To answer the questions included in a case study, you will need to reference information that is provided in the case study. Case studies might contain exhibits and other resources that provide more information about the scenario that is described in the case study. Each question is independent of the other questions in this case study.

At the end of this case study, a review screen will appear. This screen allows you to review your answers and to make changes before you move to the next section of the exam. After you begin a new section, you cannot return to this section.

To start the case study

To display the first question in this case study, click the **Next** button. Use the buttons in the left pane to explore the content of the case study before you answer the questions. Clicking these buttons displays information such as business requirements, existing environment, and problem statements. If the case study has an **All Information** tab, note that the information displayed is identical to the information displayed on the subsequent tabs. When you are ready to answer a question, click the **Question** button to return to the question.

Overview

You develop data engineering solutions for Graphics Design Institute, a global media company with offices in New York City, Manchester, Singapore, and Melbourne.

The New York office hosts SQL Server databases that stores massive amounts of customer data. The company also stores millions of images on a physical server located in the New York office. More than 2 TB of image data is added each day. The images are transferred from customer devices to the server in New York.

Many images have been placed on this server in an unorganized manner, making it difficult for editors to search images. Images should automatically have object and color tags generated. The tags must be stored in a document database, and be queried by SQL.

You are hired to design a solution that can store, transform, and visualize customer data.

Requirements Business

The company identifies the following business requirements:

- You must transfer all images and customer data to cloud storage and remove on-premises servers. You must develop an analytical processing solution for transforming customer data.
- You must develop an image object and color tagging solution. Capital expenditures must be minimized.
- Cloud resource costs must be minimized.

Technical

The solution has the following technical requirements:

- Tagging data must be uploaded to the cloud from the New York office location.
- Tagging data must be replicated to regions that are geographically close to company office locations. Image data must be stored in a single data store at minimum cost.
- Customer data must be analyzed using managed Spark clusters.
- Power BI must be used to visualize transformed customer data. All data must be backed up in case disaster recovery is required.

Security and optimization

All cloud data must be encrypted at rest and in transit. The

- solution must support: parallel processing of customer data
- hyper-scale storage of images
- global region data replication of processed image data

QUESTION 1

You need to recommend a solution for storing the image

tagging data. What should you recommend?

A. Azure File Storage
B. Azure Cosmos DB
C. Azure Blob Storage
D. Azure SQL Database
E. Azure SQL Data Warehouse

Correct Answer: C

Explanation/Reference:
Explanation:
Image data must be stored in a single data store at minimum cost.

Note: Azure Blob storage is Microsoft's object storage solution for the cloud. Blob storage is optimized for storing massive amounts of unstructured data. Unstructured data is data that does not adhere to a particular data model or definition, such as text or binary data.

Blob storage is designed for:
- Serving images or documents directly to a browser.
- Storing files for distributed access.
- Streaming video and audio. Writing to log files.
- Storing data for backup and restore, disaster recovery, and archiving.
- Storing data for analysis by an on-premises or Azure-hosted service.

Reference:
https://docs.microsoft.com/en-us/azure/storage/blobs/storage-blobs-introduction

QUESTION 2
You need to design the solution for analyzing customer data. What should you recommend?

A. Azure Databricks
B. Azure Data Lake Storage
C. Azure SQL Data Warehouse
D. Azure Cognitive Services
E. Azure Batch

Correct Answer: A

Explanation/Reference:
Explanation:
Customer data must be analyzed using managed Spark clusters. You create spark clusters through Azure Databricks.

Reference:
https://docs.microsoft.com/en-us/azure/azure-databricks/quickstart-create-databricks-workspace-portal

QUESTION 3
You need to recommend a solution for storing customer data. What should you recommend?

A. Azure SQL Data Warehouse
B. Azure Stream Analytics
C. Azure Databricks
D. Azure SQL Database

Correct Answer: C

Explanation/Reference:
Explanation: Customer data must be analyzed using managed Spark clusters. All cloud data must be encrypted at rest and in transit. The solution must support: parallel processing of customer data.

Reference:
https://www.microsoft.com/developerblog/2019/01/18/running-parallel-apache-spark-notebook-workloads-on-azure-databricks/

Testlet 3 Case study

This is a case study. Case studies are not timed separately. You can use as much exam time as you would like to complete each case. However, there may be additional case studies and sections on this exam. You must manage your time to ensure that you are able to complete all questions included on this exam in the time provided.

To answer the questions included in a case study, you will need to reference information that is provided in the case study. Case studies might contain exhibits and other resources that provide more information about the scenario that is described in the case study. Each question is independent of the other questions in this case study.

At the end of this case study, a review screen will appear. This screen allows you to review your answers and to make changes before you move to the next section of the exam. After you begin a new section, you cannot return to this section.

To start the case study
To display the first question in this case study, click the **Next** button. Use the buttons in the left pane to explore the content of the case study before you answer the questions. Clicking these buttons displays information such as business requirements, existing environment, and problem statements. If the case study has an **All Information** tab, note that the information displayed is identical to the information displayed on the subsequent tabs. When you are ready to answer a question, click the **Question** button to return to the question.

Background

Current environment

The company has the following virtual machines (VMs):

VM	Roles	Database size	VM type	Destination
CONT_SQL1	Microsoft SQL Server	2 TB	Hyper-V	Azure SQL Database
CONT_SQL2	Microsoft SQL Server	2 TB	Hyper-V	Azure SQL Database
CONT_SQL3	Microsoft SQL Server	100 GB	Hyper-V	Azure VM
CONT_SAP1	SAP	1 TB	Vmware	On-premises
CONT_SAP2	SAP	1 TB	Vmware	On-premises
CPNT_SSRS	Microsoft SQL Server Reporting Services	1 TB	Hyper-V	Azure VM

Requirements

Storage and processing

You must be able to use a file system view of data stored in a blob.
You must build an architecture that will allow Contoso to use the DB FS filesystem layer over a blob store. The architecture will need to support data files, libraries, and images.
Additionally, it must provide a web-based interface to documents that contain runnable command, visualizations, and narrative text such as a notebook.

CONT_SQL3 requires an initial scale of 35000 IOPS.
CONT_SQL1 and CONT_SQL2 must use the vCore model and should include replicas. The solution must support 8000 IOPS. The storage should be configured to optimized storage for database OLTP workloads.

Migration

- You must be able to independently scale compute and storage resources.
- You must migrate all SQL Server workloads to Azure.
- You must identify related machines in the on-premises environment, get disk size data usage information.
- Data from SQL Server must include zone redundant storage.
- You need to ensure that app components can reside on-premises while interacting with components that run in the Azure public cloud.
- SAP data must remain on-premises.
- The Azure Site Recovery (ASR) results should contain per-machine data.

Business requirements

- You must design a regional disaster recovery topology.
- The database backups have regulatory purposes and must be retained for seven years.
- CONT_SQL1 stores customers' sales data that requires ETL operations for data analysis. A solution is required that reads data from SQL, performs ETL, and outputs to Power BI. The solution should use managed clusters to minimize costs. To optimize logistics, Contoso needs to analyze customer sales data to see if certain products are tied to

specific times in the year.
- The analytics solution for customer sales data must be available during a regional outage.

Security and auditing

- Contoso requires all corporate computers to enable
- Windows Firewall. Azure servers should be able to ping other Contoso Azure servers.
- Employee PII must be encrypted in memory, in motion, and at rest. Any data encrypted by SQL Server must support equality searches, grouping, indexing, and joining on the encrypted data.
- Keys must be secured by using hardware security modules (HSMs). CONT_SQL3 must not communicate over the default ports

Cost

- All solutions must minimize cost and resources.
- The organization does not want any unexpected charges.

- The data engineers must set the SQL Data Warehouse compute resources to consume 300 DWUs.
- CONT_SQL2 is not fully utilized during non-peak hours. You must minimize resource costs for during non-peak hours.

QUESTION 1

You need to design a solution to meet the SQL Server storage requirements for CONT_SQL3. Which type of disk should you recommend?

A. Standard SSD Managed Disk
B. Premium SSD Managed Disk
C. Ultra SSD Managed Disk

Correct Answer: C

Explanation/Reference:
Explanation:
CONT_SQL3 requires an initial scale of 35000 IOPS. Ultra SSD Managed Disk Offerings

Disk size (GiB)	4	8	16	32	64	128	256	512	1,024-65,536 (in increments of 1 TiB)
IOPS range	100-1,200	100-2,400	100-4,800	100-9,600	100-19,200	100-38,400	100-76,800	100-153,600	100-160,000
Throughput Cap (MBps)	300	600	1,200	2,000	2,000	2,000	2,000	2,000	2,000

The following table provides a comparison of ultra solid-state-drives (SSD) (preview), premium SSD, standard SSD, and standard hard disk drives (HDD) for managed disks to help you decide what to use

	Ultra SSD (preview)	Premium SSD	Standard SSD	Standard HDD
Disk type	SSD	SSD	SSD	HDD
Scenario	IO-intensive workloads such as SAP HANA, top tier databases (for example, SQL, Oracle), and other transaction-heavy workloads.	Production and performance sensitive workloads	Web servers, lightly used enterprise applications and dev/test	Backup, non-critical, infrequent access
Disk size	65,536 gibibyte (GiB) (Preview)	32,767 GiB	32,767 GiB	32,767 GiB
Max throughput	2,000 MiB/s (Preview)	900 MiB/s	750 MiB/s	500 MiB/s
Max IOPS	160,000 (Preview)	20,000	6,000	2,000

Reference:

https://docs.microsoft.com/en-us/azure/virtual-
machines/windows/disks-types

QUESTION 2

You need to recommend an Azure SQL Database service tier.
What should you recommend?

A. Business Critical
B. General Purpose
C. Premium
D. Standard
E. Basic

Correct Answer: C

Explanation/Reference:
Explanation:
The data engineers must set the SQL Data Warehouse
compute resources to consume 300 DWUs.

Note: There are three architectural models that are used in
- Azure SQL Database: General Purpose/Standard
- Business Critical/Premium Hyperscale

Incorrect Answers:
A: Business Critical service tier is designed for the applications
that require low-latency responses from the underlying SSD
storage (1-2 ms in average), fast recovery if the underlying
infrastructure fails, or need to off-load reports, analytics, and
read-only queries to the free of charge readable secondary
replica of the primary database.

Reference:

https://docs.microsoft.com/en-us/azure/sql-database/sql-
database-service-tier-business-critical

QUESTION 3

You need to recommend the appropriate storage and processing solution? What should you recommend?

A. Enable auto-shrink on the database.
B. Flush the blob cache using Windows PowerShell.
C. Enable Apache Spark RDD (RDD) caching.
D. Enable Databricks IO (DBIO) caching.
E. Configure the reading speed using Azure Data Studio.

Correct Answer: C

Explanation/Reference:
Explanation:
Scenario: You must be able to use a file system view of data stored in a blob. You must build an architecture that will allow Contoso to use the DB FS filesystem layer over a blob store.

Databricks File System (DBFS) is a distributed file system installed on Azure Databricks clusters. Files in DBFS persist to Azure Blob storage, so you won't lose data even after you terminate a cluster.

The Databricks Delta cache, previously named Databricks IO (DBIO) caching, accelerates data reads by creating copies of remote files in nodes' local storage using a fast intermediate data format. The data is cached automatically whenever a file has to be fetched from a remote location. Successive reads of the same data are then performed locally, which results in significantly improved reading speed.

Reference:
https://docs.databricks.com/delta/delta-cache.html#delta-cache

Testlet 4 Case study

This is a case study. Case studies are not timed separately. You can use as much exam time as you would like to complete each case. However, there may be additional case studies and sections on this exam. You must manage your time to ensure that you are able to complete all questions included on this exam in the time provided.

To answer the questions included in a case study, you will need to reference information that is provided in the case study. Case studies might contain exhibits and other resources that provide more information about the scenario that is described in the case study. Each question is independent of the other questions in this case study.

At the end of this case study, a review screen will appear. This screen allows you to review your answers and to make changes before you move to the next section of the exam. After you begin a new section, you cannot return to this section.

To start the case study

To display the first question in this case study, click the **Next** button. Use the buttons in the left pane to explore the content of the case study before you answer the questions. Clicking these buttons displays information such as business requirements, existing environment, and problem statements. If the case study has an **All Information** tab, note that the information displayed is identical to the information displayed on the subsequent tabs. When you are ready to answer a question, click the **Question** button to return to the question.

Overview General Overview

ADatum Corporation is a medical company that has 5,000 physicians located in more than 300 hospitals across the US. The company has a medical department, a sales department, a marketing department, a medical research department, and a human resources department.

You are redesigning the application environment of ADatum.

Physical Locations

ADatum has three main offices in New York, Dallas, and Los

Angeles. The offices connect to each other by using a WAN link. Each office connects directly to the Internet. The Los Angeles office also has a datacenter that hosts all the company's applications.

Existing Environment Health Review

ADatum has a critical OLTP web application named Health Review that physicians use to track billing, patient care, and overall physician best practices.

Health Interface

ADatum has a critical application named Health Interface that receives hospital messages related to patient care and status updates. The messages are sent in batches by each hospital's enterprise relationship management (ERM) system by using a VPN. The data sent from each hospital can have varying columns and formats.

Currently, a custom C# application is used to send the data to Health Interface. The application uses deprecated libraries and a new solution must be designed for this functionality.

Health Insights

ADatum has a web-based reporting system named Health Insights that shows hospital and patient insights to physicians and business users. The data is created from the data in Health Review and Health Interface, as well as manual entries.

Database Platform

Currently, the databases for all three applications are hosted on an out-of-date VMware cluster that has a single instance of Microsoft SQL Server 2012.

Problem Statements

ADatum identifies the following issues in its current environment:

- Over time, the data received by Health Interface from the hospitals has slowed, and the number of messages has increased. When a new hospital joins ADatum, Health Interface requires a schema modification due to the lack of data standardization. The speed of batch data processing is inconsistent.

Business Requirements Business Goals

ADatum identifies the following business goals:

- Migrate the applications to Azure whenever possible.
- Minimize the development effort required to perform data movement.
- Provide continuous integration and deployment for development, test, and production environments.
- Provide faster access to the applications and the data and provide more consistent application performance.
- Minimize the number of services required to perform data processing, development, scheduling, monitoring, and the operationalizing of pipelines.

Health Review Requirements

ADatum identifies the following requirements for the Health Review application:

- Ensure that sensitive health data is encrypted at rest and in transit.
- Tag all the sensitive health data in Health Review. The data will be used for auditing.

Health Interface Requirements

ADatum identifies the following requirements for the Health Interface application:

- Upgrade to a data storage solution that will provide flexible schemas and increased throughput for writing data. Data must be regionally located close to each hospital, and reads must display be the most recent committed version of an item.
- Reduce the amount of time it takes to add data from new hospitals to Health Interface. Support a more scalable batch processing solution in Azure.
- Reduce the amount of development effort to rewrite existing

SQL queries.

Health Insights Requirements

ADatum identifies the following requirements for the Health
Insights application:

- The analysis of events must be performed over time by
  using an organizational date dimension table.
- The data from Health Interface and Health Review must be
  available in Health Insights within 15 minutes of being
  committed.
- The new Health Insights application must be built on a
  massively parallel processing (MPP) architecture that will
  support the high performance of joins on large fact tables.

QUESTION 1

You need to design a solution that meets the business requirements of Health Insights. What should you include in the recommendation?

A. Azure Cosmos DB that uses the Gremlin

B. Azure Data Factory

C. Azure Cosmos DB that uses the SQL API

D. Azure Databricks

Correct Answer: D

Explanation/Reference:
Explanation:
Azure SQL Data Warehouse is a cloud-based enterprise data warehouse that leverages massively parallel processing (MPP) to quickly run complex queries across petabytes of data. Use SQL Data Warehouse as a key component of a big data solution.

You can access Azure SQL Data Warehouse (SQL DW) from Databricks using the SQL Data Warehouse connector (referred to as the SQL DW connector), a data source implementation for Apache Spark that uses Azure Blob Storage, and PolyBase in SQL DW to transfer large volumes of data efficiently between a Databricks cluster and a SQL DW instance.

Scenario: ADatum identifies the following requirements for the Health Insights application:

- The new Health Insights application must be built on a massively parallel processing (MPP) architecture that will support the high performance of joins on large fact tables

Reference:
https://docs.databricks.com/data/data-sources/azure/sql-data-warehouse.html

QUESTION 2

You need to recommend a solution that meets the data platform requirements of Health Interface. The solution must minimize redevelopment efforts for the application.

What should you include in the recommendation?

A. Azure SQL Data Warehouse
B. Azure SQL Database
C. Azure Cosmos DB that uses the SQL API
D. Azure Cosmos DB that uses the Table API

Correct Answer: C

Explanation/Reference:
Explanation:

Scenario: ADatum identifies the following requirements for the
- Health Interface application: Reduce the amount of development effort to rewrite existing SQL queries.
- Upgrade to a data storage solution that will provide flexible schemas and increased throughput for writing data. Data must be regionally located close to each hospital, and reads must display be the most recent committed version of an item.
- Reduce the amount of time it takes to add data from new hospitals to Health Interface. Support a more scalable batch processing solution in Azure.

QUESTION 3

Which consistency level should you use for Health Interface?

A. Consistent Prefix

B. Session

C. Bounded Staleness

D. Strong

Correct Answer: D

Explanation/Reference:
Explanation:
Scenario: ADatum identifies the following requirements for the Health Interface application:

- ..reads must display be the most recent committed version of an item.

Azure Cosmos DB consistency levels include:
Strong: Strong consistency offers a linearizability guarantee. Linearizability refers to serving requests concurrently. The reads are guaranteed to return the most recent committed version of an item. A client never sees an uncommitted or partial write. Users are always guaranteed to read the latest committed write.

Reference:
https://docs.microsoft.com/en-us/azure/cosmos-db/consistency-levels

Testlet 5 Overview

You are a data engineer for Trey Research. The company is close to completing a joint project with the government to build smart highways infrastructure across North America. This involves the placement of sensors and cameras to measure traffic flow, car speed, and vehicle details.

You have been asked to design a cloud solution that will meet the business and technical requirements of the smart highway.

Solution components Telemetry Capture

The telemetry capture system records each time a vehicle passes in front of a sensor. The sensors run on a custom embedded operating system and record the following telemetry data:

- Time
- Location in latitude and longitude
- Speed in kilometers per hour (kmph)
- Length of vehicle in meters

Visual Monitoring

The visual monitoring system is a network of approximately 1,000 cameras placed near highways that capture images of vehicle traffic every 2 seconds. The cameras record high resolution images. Each image is approximately 3 MB in size.

Requirements: Business

The company identifies the following business requirements:

- External vendors must be able to perform custom analysis of data using machine learning technologies.
- You must display a dashboard on the operations status page that displays the following metrics: telemetry, volume, and processing latency.
- Traffic data must be made available to the Government Planning Department for the purpose of modeling changes to the highway system.
- The traffic data will be used in conjunction with other data such as information about events such as sporting events, weather conditions, and population statistics. External data

used during the modeling is stored in on-premises SQL Server 2016 databases and CSV files stored in an Azure Data Lake Storage Gen2 storage account. Information about vehicles that have been detected as going over the speed limit during the last 30 minutes must be available to law enforcement officers.
Several law enforcement organizations may respond to speeding vehicles.

- The solution must allow for searches of vehicle images by license plate to support law enforcement investigations. Searches must be able to be performed using a query language and must support fuzzy searches to compensate for license plate detection errors.

Requirements: Security

The solution must meet the following security requirements:

- External vendors must not have direct access to sensor data or images.
- Images produced by the vehicle monitoring solution must be deleted after one month. You must minimize costs associated with deleting images from the data store.
- Unauthorized usage of data must be detected in real time. Unauthorized usage is determined by looking for unusual usage patterns.
- All changes to Azure resources used by the solution must be recorded and stored. Data must be provided to the security team for incident response purposes.

Requirements: Sensor data

You must write all telemetry data to the closest Azure region. The sensors used for the telemetry capture system have a small amount of memory available and so must write data as quickly as possible to avoid losing telemetry data.

QUESTION 1
You need to design the storage for the visual monitoring system. Which storage solution should you recommend?

A. Azure Blob storage
B. Azure Table storage
C. Azure SQL database
D. Azure Media Services

Correct Answer: A

Explanation/Reference:
Explanation:
Azure Blobs: A massively scalable object store for text and binary data.

Scenario:
- The visual monitoring system is a network of approximately 1,000 cameras placed near highways that capture images of vehicle traffic every 2 seconds. The cameras record high resolution images. Each image is approximately 3 MB in size.
- The solution must allow for searches of vehicle images by license plate to support law enforcement investigations. Searches must be able to be performed using a query language and must support fuzzy searches to compensate for license plate detection errors.

Incorrect Answers:
B: Azure Tables: A NoSQL store for schemaless storage of structured data.

D: Microsoft Azure Media Services (AMS) is a leading full-service media platform for securely delivering live and on-demand video to virtually any device.

Reference:
https://docs.microsoft.com/en-us/azure/storage/common/storage-introduction

QUESTION 2

You need to design the storage for the telemetry capture system. What storage solution should you use in the design?

A. Azure SQL Synapse Analytics
B. Azure Databricks
C. Azure Cosmos DB

Correct Answer: C

Explanation/Reference:
Explanation:
Azure Cosmos DB is a globally distributed database service. You can associate any number of Azure regions with your Azure Cosmos account and your data is automatically and transparently replicated.

Scenario:
Telemetry Capture
The telemetry capture system records each time a vehicle passes in front of a sensor. The sensors run on a custom embedded operating system and record the following telemetry data:
- Time
- Location in latitude and longitude
- Speed in kilometers per hour (kmph)
- Length of vehicle in meters

You must write all telemetry data to the closest Azure region. The sensors used for the telemetry capture system have a small amount of memory available and so must write data as quickly as possible to avoid losing telemetry data.

Reference:
https://docs.microsoft.com/en-us/azure/cosmos-db/regional-presence

QUESTION 3

You need to design the solution for the government planning department. Which services should you include in the design?

A. Azure Synapse Analytics and Elastic Queries
B. Azure SQL Database and Polybase
C. Azure Synapse Analytics and Polybase
D. Azure SQL Database and Elastic Queries

Correct Answer: C

Explanation/Reference:
Explanation:
PolyBase is a new feature in SQL Server 2016. It is used to query relational and non-relational databases (NoSQL) such as CSV files.

Scenario: Traffic data must be made available to the Government Planning Department for the purpose of modeling changes to the highway system. The traffic data will be used in conjunction with other data such as information about events such as sporting events, weather conditions, and population statistics. External data used during the modeling is stored in on-premises SQL Server 2016 databases and CSV files stored in an Azure Data Lake Storage Gen2 storage account.

Reference:
https://www.sqlshack.com/sql-server-2016-polybase-tutorial/

Testlet 6 Case study

This is a case study. Case studies are not timed separately. You can use as much exam time as you would like to complete each case. However, there may be additional case studies and sections on this exam. You must manage your time to ensure that you are able to complete all questions included on this exam in the time provided.

To answer the questions included in a case study, you will need to reference information that is provided in the case study. Case studies might contain exhibits and other resources that provide more information about the scenario that is described in the case study. Each question is independent of the other questions in this case study.

At the end of this case study, a review screen will appear. This screen allows you to review your answers and to make changes before you move to the next section of the exam. After you begin a new section, you cannot return to this section.

To start the case study
To display the first question in this case study, click the **Next** button. Use the buttons in the left pane to explore the content of the case study before you answer the questions. Clicking these buttons displays information such as business requirements, existing environment, and problem statements. If the case study has an **All Information** tab, note that the information displayed is identical to the information displayed on the subsequent tabs. When you are ready to answer a question, click the **Question** button to return to the question.

Overview

Litware, Inc. owns and operates 300 convenience stores across the US. The company sells a variety of packaged foods and drinks, as well as a variety of prepared foods, such as sandwiches and pizzas.

Litware has a loyalty club whereby members can get daily discounts on specific items by providing their membership number at checkout.

Litware employs business analysts who prefer to analyze data by using Microsoft Power BI, and data scientists who prefer

analyzing data in Azure Databricks notebooks.

Requirements. Business Goals

Litware wants to create a new analytics environment in Azure to meet the following requirements:

- See inventory levels across the stores. Data must be updated as close to real time as possible.
- Execute ad hoc analytical queries on historical data to identify whether the loyalty club discounts increase sales of the discounted products. Every four hours, notify store employees about how many prepared food items to produce based on historical demand from the sales data.

Requirements. Technical Requirements

Litware identifies the following technical requirements:

- Minimize the number of different Azure services needed to achieve the business goals
- Use platform as a service (PaaS) offerings whenever possible and avoid having to provision virtual machines that must be managed by Litware.
- Ensure that the analytical data store is accessible only to the company's on-premises network and Azure services.
- Use Azure Active Directory (Azure AD) authentication whenever possible. Use the principle of least privilege when designing security.
- Stage inventory data in Azure Data Lake Storage Gen2 before loading the data into the analytical data store.
- Litware wants to remove transient data from Data Lake Storage once the data is no longer in use.
- Files that have a modified date that is older than 14 days must be removed.
- Limit the business analysts' access to customer contact information, such as phone numbers, because this type of data is not analytically relevant.
- Ensure that you can quickly restore a copy of the analytical data store within one hour in the event of corruption or accidental deletion.

Requirements. Planned Environment

Litware plans to implement the following environment:

- The application development team will create an Azure event hub to receive real-time sales data, including store number, date, time, product ID, customer loyalty number, price, and discount amount, from the point of sale (POS) system and output the data to data storage in Azure.
- Customer data, including name, contact information, and loyalty number, comes from Salesforce and can be imported into Azure once every eight hours. Row modified dates are not trusted in the source table.
- Product data, including product ID, name, and category, comes from Salesforce and can be imported into Azure once every eight hours. Row modified dates are not trusted in the source table.
- Daily inventory data comes from a Microsoft SQL server located on a private network.
- Litware currently has 5 TB of historical sales data and 100 GB of customer data. The company expects approximately 100 GB of new data per month for the next year.
- Litware will build a custom application named FoodPrep to provide store employees with the calculation results of how many prepared food items to produce every four hours.
- Litware does not plan to implement Azure ExpressRoute or a VPN between the on-premises network and Azure.

QUESTION 1

Which Azure service should you recommend for the analytical data store so that the business analysts and data scientists can execute ad hoc queries as quickly as possible?

A. Azure Data Lake Storage Gen2
B. Azure Cosmos DB
C. Azure SQL Database
D. Azure Synapse Analytics

Correct Answer: A

Explanation/Reference:
Explanation:
There are several differences between a data lake and a data warehouse. Data structure, ideal users, processing methods, and the overall purpose of the data are the key differentiators.

	Data Lake	Data Warehouse
Data Structure	Raw	Processed
Purpose of Data	Not Yet Determined	Currently In Use
Users	Data Scientists	Business Professionals
Accessibility	Highly accessible and quick to update	More complicated and costly to make changes

Scenario: Litware employs business analysts who prefer to analyze data by using Microsoft Power BI, and data scientists who prefer analyzing data in Azure Databricks notebooks.

Note: Azure Synapse Analytics formerly known as Azure SQL Data Warehouse.

QUESTION 1

You are designing an HDInsight/Hadoop cluster solution that uses Azure Data Lake Gen1 Storage. The solution requires POSIX permissions and enables diagnostics logging for auditing.
You need to recommend solutions that optimize storage.
Proposed Solution: Ensure that files stored are larger than 250MB. Does the solution meet the goal?

A. Yes
B. No

Correct Answer: A

Explanation/Reference:
Explanation:
Depending on what services and workloads are using the data, a good size to consider for files is 256 MB or greater. If the file sizes cannot be batched when landing in Data Lake Storage Gen1, you can have a separate compaction job that combines these files into larger ones.

Note: POSIX permissions and auditing in Data Lake Storage Gen1 comes with an overhead that becomes apparent when working with numerous small files. As a best practice, you must batch your data into larger files versus writing thousands or millions of small files to Data Lake Storage Gen1. Avoiding small file sizes can have multiple benefits, such as:
- Lowering the authentication checks across multiple files
- Reduced open file connections
- Faster copying/replication
- Fewer files to process when updating Data Lake Storage Gen1 POSIX permissions

Reference:
https://docs.microsoft.com/en-us/azure/data-lake-store/data-lake-store-best-practices

QUESTION 2

You are designing an HDInsight/Hadoop cluster solution that uses Azure Data Lake Gen1 Storage. The solution requires POSIX permissions and enables diagnostics logging for auditing.
You need to recommend solutions that optimize storage.

Proposed Solution: Implement compaction jobs to combine small files into larger files. Does the solution meet the goal?
A. Yes
B. No

Correct Answer: A

Explanation/Reference:
Explanation:
Depending on what services and workloads are using the data, a good size to consider for files is 256 MB or greater. If the file sizes cannot be batched when landing in Data Lake Storage Gen1, you can have a separate compaction job that combines these files into larger ones.

Note: POSIX permissions and auditing in Data Lake Storage Gen1 comes with an overhead that becomes apparent when working with numerous small files. As a best practice, you must batch your data into larger files versus writing thousands or millions of small files to Data Lake Storage Gen1. Avoiding small file sizes can have multiple benefits, such as:
- Lowering the authentication checks across multiple files
- Reduced open file connections
- Faster copying/replication
- Fewer files to process when updating Data Lake Storage Gen1 POSIX permissions

Reference:
https://docs.microsoft.com/en-us/azure/data-lake-store/data-lake-store-best-practices

QUESTION 3

You are designing an HDInsight/Hadoop cluster solution that uses Azure Data Lake Gen1 Storage. The solution requires POSIX permissions and enables diagnostics logging for auditing.
You need to recommend solutions that optimize storage.

Proposed Solution: Ensure that files stored are smaller than 250MB. Does the solution meet the goal?

A. Yes
B. No

Correct Answer: B

Explanation/Reference:
Explanation:
Ensure that files stored are larger, not smaller than 250MB.
You can have a separate compaction job that combines these files into larger ones.

Note: The file POSIX permissions and auditing in Data Lake Storage Gen1 comes with an overhead that becomes apparent when working with numerous small files. As a best practice, you must batch your data into larger files versus writing thousands or millions of small files to Data Lake Storage Gen1. Avoiding small file sizes can have multiple benefits, such as:
- Lowering the authentication checks across multiple files
- Reduced open file connections
- Faster copying/replication
- Fewer files to process when updating Data Lake Storage Gen1 POSIX permissions

Reference:
https://docs.microsoft.com/en-us/azure/data-lake-store/data-lake-store-best-practices

QUESTION 4

You are designing an Azure SQL Database that will use elastic pools. You plan to store data about customers in a table. Each record uses a value for CustomerID. You need to recommend a strategy to partition data based on values in CustomerID. Proposed Solution: Separate data into customer regions by using vertical partitioning. Does the solution meet the goal?

A. Yes
B. No

Correct Answer: B

Explanation/Reference:
Explanation:
Vertical partitioning is used for cross-database queries. Instead we should use Horizontal Partitioning, which also is called charding.

Reference:
https://docs.microsoft.com/en-us/azure/sql-database/sql-database-elastic-query-overview

QUESTION 5

You are designing an Azure SQL Database that will use elastic pools. You plan to store data about customers in a table. Each record uses a value for CustomerID. You need to recommend a strategy to partition data based on values in CustomerID. Proposed Solution: Separate data into customer regions by using horizontal partitioning. Does the solution meet the goal?

A. Yes
B. No

Correct Answer: B

Explanation/Reference:
Explanation:
We should use Horizontal Partitioning through Sharding, not divide through regions.

Note: Horizontal Partitioning - Sharding: Data is partitioned horizontally to distribute rows across a scaled out data tier. With this approach, the schema is identical on all participating databases. This approach is also called "sharding". Sharding can be performed and managed using (1) the elastic database tools libraries or (2) self-sharding. An elastic query is used to query or compile reports across many shards.

Reference:
https://docs.microsoft.com/en-us/azure/sql-database/sql-database-elastic-query-overview

QUESTION 6

You are designing an Azure SQL Database that will use elastic pools. You plan to store data about customers in a table. Each record uses a value for CustomerID. You need to recommend a strategy to partition data based on values in CustomerID. Proposed Solution: Separate data into shards by using horizontal partitioning. Does the solution meet the goal?

A. Yes
B. No

Correct Answer: A

Explanation/Reference:
Explanation:
Horizontal Partitioning - Sharding: Data is partitioned horizontally to distribute rows across a scaled out data tier. With this approach, the schema is identical on all participating databases. This approach is also called "sharding". Sharding can be performed and managed using (1) the elastic database tools libraries or (2) self- sharding. An elastic query is used to query or compile reports across many shards.

Reference:
https://docs.microsoft.com/en-us/azure/sql-database/sql-database-elastic-query-overview

QUESTION 7

You are evaluating data storage solutions to support a new application.

You need to recommend a data storage solution that represents data by using nodes and relationships in graph structures. Which data storage solution should you recommend?

A. Blob Storage
B. Cosmos DB
C. Data Lake Store
D. HDInsight

Correct Answer: B

Explanation/Reference:
Explanation:
For large graphs with lots of entities and relationships, you can perform very complex analyses very quickly. Many graph databases provide a query language that you can use to traverse a network of relationships efficiently.

Relevant Azure service: Cosmos DB Reference:
https://docs.microsoft.com/en-us/azure/architecture/guide/technology-choices/data-store-overview

QUESTION 8

You are designing a data processing solution that will implement the lambda architecture pattern. The solution will use Spark running on HDInsight for data processing.

You need to recommend a data storage technology for the solution.

Which two technologies should you recommend? Each correct answer presents a complete solution.

NOTE: Each correct selection is worth one point.

A. Azure Cosmos DB

B. Azure Service Bus

C. Azure Storage Queue

D. Apache Cassandra

E. Kafka HDInsight

Correct Answer: AE

Explanation/Reference:
Explanation:
To implement a lambda architecture on Azure, you can combine the following technologies to accelerate real-time big data analytics:

- Azure Cosmos DB, the industry's first globally distributed, multi-model database service.
- Apache Spark for Azure HDInsight, a processing framework that runs large-scale data analytics applications Azure Cosmos DB change feed, which streams new data to the batch layer for HDInsight to process
- The Spark to Azure Cosmos DB Connector

E: You can use Apache Spark to stream data into or out of Apache Kafka on HDInsight using DStreams.

Reference:
https://docs.microsoft.com/en-us/azure/cosmos-db/lambda-architecture

QUESTION 9

A company manufactures automobile parts. The company installs IoT sensors on manufacturing machinery. You must design a solution that analyzes data from the sensors.

You need to recommend a solution that meets the following requirements:

- Data must be analyzed in real-time.
- Data queries must be deployed using continuous integration.
- Data must be visualized by using charts and graphs.
- Data must be available for ETL operations in the future.
- The solution must support high-volume data ingestion.

Which three actions should you recommend? Each correct answer presents part of the solution.

NOTE: Each correct selection is worth one point.

A. Use Azure Analysis Services to query the data. Output query results to Power BI.

B. Configure an Azure Event Hub to capture data to Azure Data Lake Storage.

C. Develop an Azure Stream Analytics application that queries the data and outputs to Power BI. Use Azure Data Factory to deploy the Azure Stream Analytics application.

D. Develop an application that sends the IoT data to an Azure Event Hub.

E. Develop an Azure Stream Analytics application that queries the data and outputs to Power BI. Use Azure Pipelines to deploy the Azure Stream Analytics application.

F. Develop an application that sends the IoT data to an Azure Data Lake Storage container.

Correct Answer: BCD

QUESTION 10
You are designing an Azure Databricks interactive cluster.
You need to ensure that the cluster meets the following
requirements:

- Enable auto-termination
- Retain cluster configuration indefinitely after cluster termination.

What should you recommend?

A. Start the cluster after it is terminated.

B. Pin the cluster

C. Clone the cluster after it is terminated.

D. Terminate the cluster manually at process completion.

Correct Answer: B

Explanation/Reference:
Explanation:
To keep an interactive cluster configuration even after it has
been terminated for more than 30 days, an administrator can
pin a cluster to the cluster list.

Reference:
https://docs.azuredatabricks.net/user-
guide/clusters/terminate.html

QUESTION 11

You are designing a solution for a company. The solution will use model training for objective classification. You need to design the solution.
What should you recommend?

A. an Azure Cognitive Services application
B. a Spark Streaming job
C. interactive Spark queries
D. Power BI models
E. a Spark application that uses Spark MLib.

Correct Answer: E

Explanation/Reference:
Explanation:
Spark in SQL Server big data cluster enables AI and machine learning.
You can use Apache Spark MLlib to create a machine learning application to do simple predictive analysis on an open dataset.

- MLlib is a core Spark library that provides many utilities useful for machine learning tasks, including utilities that are suitable for: Classification
- Regression Clustering Topic modeling
- Singular value decomposition (SVD) and principal component analysis (PCA) Hypothesis testing and calculating sample statistics

Reference:
https://docs.microsoft.com/en-us/azure/hdinsight/spark/apache-spark-machine-learning-mllib-ipython

QUESTION 12

A company stores data in multiple types of cloud-based databases.

You need to design a solution to consolidate data into a single relational database. Ingestion of data will occur at set times each day. What should you recommend?

A. SQL Server Migration Assistant
B. SQL Data Sync
C. Azure Data Factory
D. Azure Database Migration Service
E. Data Migration Assistant

Correct Answer: C

Explanation/Reference:
Explanation:
Incorrect Answers:
D: Azure Database Migration Service is used to migrate on-premises SQL Server databases to the cloud.

Reference:
https://docs.microsoft.com/en-us/azure/data-factory/introduction

https://azure.microsoft.com/en-us/blog/operationalize-azure-databricks-notebooks-using-data-factory/

https://azure.microsoft.com/en-us/blog/data-ingestion-into-azure-at-scale-made-easier-with-latest-enhancements-to-adf-copy-data-tool/

QUESTION 13

You are designing an application. You plan to use Azure SQL Database to support the application.

The application will extract data from the Azure SQL Database and create text documents. The text documents will be placed into a cloud-based storage solution. The text storage solution must be accessible from an SMB network share.

You need to recommend a data storage solution for the text documents. Which Azure data storage type should you recommend?

A. Queue
B. Files
C. Blob
D. Table

Correct Answer: B

Explanation/Reference:
Explanation:
Azure Files enables you to set up highly available network file shares that can be accessed by using the standard Server Message Block (SMB) protocol.

Incorrect Answers:
A: The Azure Queue service is used to store and retrieve messages. It is generally used to store lists of messages to be processed asynchronously.
C: Blob storage is optimized for storing massive amounts of unstructured data, such as text or binary data. Blob storage can be accessed via HTTP or HTTPS but not via SMB.
D: Azure Table storage is used to store large amounts of structured data. Azure tables are ideal for storing structured, non-relational data.

Reference:
https://docs.microsoft.com/en-us/azure/storage/common/storage-introduction https://docs.microsoft.com/en-us/azure/storage/tables/table-storage-overview

QUESTION 14

You are designing an application that will have an Azure virtual machine. The virtual machine will access an Azure SQL database. The database will not be accessible from the Internet

You need to recommend a solution to provide the required level of access to the database. What should you include in the recommendation?

A. Deploy an On-premises data gateway.
B. Add a virtual network to the Azure SQL server that hosts the database.
C. Add an application gateway to the virtual network that contains the Azure virtual machine.
D. Add a virtual network gateway to the virtual network that contains the Azure virtual machine.

Correct Answer: B

Explanation/Reference:
Explanation:
When you create an Azure virtual machine (VM), you must create a virtual network (VNet) or use an existing VNet. You also need to decide how your VMs are intended to be accessed on the VNet.

Incorrect Answers:

C: Azure Application Gateway is a web traffic load balancer that enables you to manage traffic to your web applications.

D: A VPN gateway is a specific type of virtual network gateway that is used to send encrypted traffic between an Azure virtual network and an on-premises location over the public Internet.

Reference:
https://docs.microsoft.com/en-us/azure/virtual-machines/windows/network-overview

QUESTION 15

You are designing a data store that will store organizational information for a company. The data will be used to identify the relationships between users. The data will be stored in an Azure Cosmos DB database and will contain several million objects.

You need to recommend which API to use for the database. The API must minimize the complexity to query the user relationships. The solution must support fast traversals.

Which API should you recommend?

A. MongoDB
B. Table
C. Gremlin
D. Cassandra

Correct Answer: C

Explanation/Reference:
Explanation:
Gremlin features fast queries and traversals with the most widely adopted graph query standard.

Reference:
https://docs.microsoft.com/th-th/azure/cosmos-db/graph-introduction?view=azurermps-5.7.0

QUESTION 16

You need to recommend a storage solution to store flat files and columnar optimized files. The solution must meet the following requirements:

- Store standardized data that data scientists will explore in a curated folder. Ensure that applications cannot access the curated folder.
- Store staged data for import to applications in a raw folder.
- Provide data scientists with access to specific folders in the raw folder and all the content the curated folder.

Which storage solution should you recommend?

A. Azure SQL Data Warehouse
B. Azure Blob storage
C. Azure Data Lake Storage Gen2
D. Azure SQL Database

Correct Answer: B

Explanation/Reference:
Explanation:
Azure Blob Storage containers is a general purpose object store for a wide variety of storage scenarios. Blobs are stored in containers, which are similar to folders.

Incorrect Answers:
C: Azure Data Lake Storage is an optimized storage for big data analytics workloads.

Reference:
https://docs.microsoft.com/en-us/azure/architecture/data-guide/technology-choices/data-storage

QUESTION 17

Your company is an online retailer that can have more than 100 million orders during a 24-hour period, 95 percent of which are placed between 16:30 and 17:00. All the orders are in US dollars. The current product line contains the following three item categories:

- Games with 15,123 items Books with 35,312 items Pens with 6,234 items
- You are designing an Azure Cosmos DB data solution for a collection named Orders Collection. The following documents is a typical order in Orders Collection.

```
"OrderTime": "16:35",
"id": " d0379ca2-f912-5h7f-k159-340ffa1z18e4"
"Item": {
    "id": "08g17u57-1j58-6511-4x65-
    2qb5bf723u5s",
    "Title": "Living the Data Dream",
    "Category": "Books",
    "PurchasePrice": 12.56,
    "Currency": "USD"
}
```

Order Collection is expected to have a balanced read/write-intensive workload. Which partition key provides the most efficient throughput?

A. Item/Category

B. OrderTime

C. Item/Currency

D. Item/id

Correct Answer: A

Explanation/Reference:
Explanation:
Choose a partition key that has a wide range of values and access patterns that are evenly spread across logical partitions. This helps spread the data and the activity in your container across the set of logical partitions, so that resources for data storage and throughput can be distributed across the logical

partitions.

Choose a partition key that spreads the workload evenly across all partitions and evenly over time. Your choice of partition key should balance the need for efficient partition queries and transactions against the goal of distributing items across multiple partitions to achieve scalability.

Candidates for partition keys might include properties that appear frequently as a filter in your queries. Queries can be efficiently routed by including the partition key in the filter predicate.

Reference:
https://docs.microsoft.com/en-us/azure/cosmos-db/partitioning-overview#choose-partitionkey

QUESTION 18

You have a MongoDB database that you plan to migrate to an Azure Cosmos DB account that uses the MongoDB API. During testing, you discover that the migration takes longer than expected.

You need to recommend a solution that will reduce the amount of time it takes to migrate the data.

What are two possible recommendations to achieve this goal? Each correct answer presents a complete solution.

NOTE: Each correct selection is worth one point.

A. Increase the Request Units (RUs).
B. Turn off indexing.
C. Add a write region.
D. Create unique indexes.
E. Create compound indexes.

Correct Answer: AB

Explanation/Reference:
Explanation:
A: Increase the throughput during the migration by increasing the Request Units (RUs).

For customers that are migrating many collections within a database, it is strongly recommend to configure database-level throughput. You must make this choice when you create the database. The minimum database-level throughput capacity is 400 RU/sec. Each collection sharing database-level throughput requires at least 100 RU/sec.

B: By default, Azure Cosmos DB indexes all your data fields upon ingestion. You can modify the indexing policy in Azure Cosmos DB at any time. In fact, it is often recommended to turn off indexing when migrating data, and then turn it back on when the data is already in CosmosDB.

Reference:
https://docs.microsoft.com/bs-latn-ba/Azure/cosmos-db/mongodb-pre-migration

QUESTION 19
You need to recommend a storage solution for a sales system that will receive thousands of small files per minute. The files will be in JSON, text, and CSV formats. The files will be processed and transformed before they are loaded into a data warehouse in Azure Synapse Analytics. The files must be stored and secured in folders.

Which storage solution should you recommend?

A. Azure Data Lake Storage Gen2
B. Azure Cosmos DB
C. Azure SQL Database
D. Azure Blob storage

Correct Answer: A

Explanation/Reference:
Explanation:
Azure provides several solutions for working with CSV and JSON files, depending on your needs. The primary landing place for these files is either Azure Storage or Azure Data Lake Store.1

Azure Data Lake Storage is an optimized storage for big data

analytics workloads. Incorrect Answers:
D: Azure Blob Storage containers is a general purpose object store for a wide variety of storage scenarios. Blobs are stored in containers, which are similar to folders.

Reference:
https://docs.microsoft.com/en-us/azure/architecture/data-guide/scenarios/csv-and-json

QUESTION 20

You are designing an Azure Cosmos DB database that will support vertices and edges. Which Cosmos DB API should you include in the design?

A. SQL
B. Cassandra
C. Gremlin
D. Table

Correct Answer: C

Explanation/Reference:

Explanation:
The Azure Cosmos DB Gremlin API can be used to store massive graphs with billions of vertices and edges.

Reference:
https://docs.microsoft.com/en-us/azure/cosmos-db/graph-introduction

QUESTION 21

You are designing a big data storage solution. The solution must meet the following requirements:

- Provide unlimited account sizes.
- Support a hierarchical file system.
- Be optimized for parallel analytics workloads.

Which storage solution should you use?

A. Azure Data Lake Storage Gen2
B. Azure Blob storage
C. Apache HBase in Azure HDInsight
D. Azure Cosmos DB

Correct Answer: A

Explanation/Reference:
Explanation:
Azure Data Lake Storage is optimized performance for parallel analytics workloads

A key mechanism that allows Azure Data Lake Storage Gen2 to provide file system performance at object storage scale and prices is the addition of a hierarchical namespace. This allows the collection of objects/files within an account to be organized into a hierarchy of directories and nested subdirectories in the same way that the file system on your computer is organized.

Reference:
https://docs.microsoft.com/en-us/azure/storage/blobs/data-lake-storage-namespace

QUESTION 22

You plan to store delimited text files in an Azure Data Lake
Storage account that will be organized into department folders.
You need to configure data access so that users see only the
files in their respective department folder.

Solution: From the storage account, you enable a hierarchical
namespace, and you use RBAC. Does this meet the goal?

A. Yes
B. No

Correct Answer: B

Explanation/Reference:
Explanation:
Disable the hierarchical namespace. And instead of RBAC use
access control lists (ACLs).

Note: Azure Data Lake Storage implements an access control
model that derives from HDFS, which in turn derives from the
POSIX access control model. Blob container ACLs does not
support the hierarchical namespace, so it must be disabled.

Reference:
https://docs.microsoft.com/en-us/azure/storage/blobs/data-lake-
storage-known-issues https://docs.microsoft.com/en-
us/azure/data-lake-store/data-lake-store-access-control

QUESTION 23

You plan to store delimited text files in an Azure Data Lake Storage account that will be organized into department folders. You need to configure data access so that users see only the files in their respective department folder.

Solution: From the storage account, you disable a hierarchical namespace, and you use RBAC. Does this meet the goal?

A. Yes
B. No

Correct Answer: B

Explanation/Reference:
Explanation:
Instead of RBAC use access control lists (ACLs).

Note: Azure Data Lake Storage implements an access control model that derives from HDFS, which in turn derives from the POSIX access control model. Blob container ACLs does not support the hierarchical namespace, so it must be disabled.

Reference:
https://docs.microsoft.com/en-us/azure/storage/blobs/data-lake-storage-known-issues https://docs.microsoft.com/en-us/azure/data-lake-store/data-lake-store-access-control

QUESTION 24

You plan to store delimited text files in an Azure Data Lake Storage account that will be organized into department folders. You need to configure data access so that users see only the files in their respective department folder.

Solution: From the storage account, you disable a hierarchical namespace, and you use access control lists (ACLs). Does this meet the goal?

A. Yes
B. No

Correct Answer: A

Explanation/Reference:
Explanation:
Azure Data Lake Storage implements an access control model that derives from HDFS, which in turn derives from the POSIX access control model. Blob container ACLs does not support the hierarchical namespace, so it must be disabled.

Reference:
https://docs.microsoft.com/en-us/azure/storage/blobs/data-lake-storage-known-issues https://docs.microsoft.com/en-us/azure/data-lake-store/data-lake-store-access-control

QUESTION 25
You plan to store 100 GB of data used by a line-of-business
(LOB) app.

You need to recommend a data storage solution for the data.
The solution must meet the following requirements:

- Minimize storage costs.
- Natively support relational queries.
- Provide a recovery time objective (RTO) of less than one
  minute

What should you include in the recommendation?

A. Azure Cosmos DB
B. Azure SQL Database
C. Azure SQL Data Warehouse
D. Azure Blob storage

Correct Answer: D

Explanation/Reference:
Incorrect Answers:
A: Azure Cosmos DB would require an SQL API.

QUESTION 26

You are designing a data storage solution for a database that is expected to grow to 50 TB. The usage pattern is singleton inserts, singleton updates, and reporting.

Which storage solution should you use?

A. Azure SQL Database elastic pools
B. Azure SQL Data Warehouse
C. Azure Cosmos DB that uses the Gremlin API
D. Azure SQL Database Hyperscale

Correct Answer: D

Explanation/Reference:
Explanation:
A Hyperscale database is an Azure SQL database in the Hyperscale service tier that is backed by the Hyperscale scale-out storage technology. A Hyperscale database supports up to 100 TB of data and provides high throughput and performance, as well as rapid scaling to adapt to the workload requirements. Scaling is transparent to the application – connectivity, query processing, etc. work like any other Azure SQL database.

Incorrect Answers:
A: SQL Database elastic pools are a simple, cost-effective solution for managing and scaling multiple databases that have varying and unpredictable usage demands. The databases in an elastic pool are on a single Azure SQL Database server and share a set number of resources at a set price. Elastic pools in Azure SQL Database enable SaaS developers to optimize the price performance for a group of databases within a prescribed budget while delivering performance elasticity for each database.
B: Rather than SQL Data Warehouse, consider other options for operational (OLTP) workloads that have large numbers of singleton selects.

Reference:
https://docs.microsoft.com/en-us/azure/sql-database/sql-database-service-tier-hyperscale-faq

Testlet 1 Case study

This is a case study. Case studies are not timed separately. You can use as much exam time as you would like to complete each case. However, there may be additional case studies and sections on this exam. You must manage your time to ensure that you are able to complete all questions included on this exam in the time provided.

To answer the questions included in a case study, you will need to reference information that is provided in the case study. Case studies might contain exhibits and other resources that provide more information about the scenario that is described in the case study. Each question is independent of the other questions in this case study.

At the end of this case study, a review screen will appear. This screen allows you to review your answers and to make changes before you move to the next section of the exam. After you begin a new section, you cannot return to this section.

To start the case study

To display the first question in this case study, click the **Next** button. Use the buttons in the left pane to explore the content of the case study before you answer the questions. Clicking these buttons displays information such as business requirements, existing environment, and problem statements. If the case study has an **All Information** tab, note that the information displayed is identical to the information displayed on the subsequent tabs. When you are ready to answer a question, click the **Question** button to return to the question.

Background

Trey Research is a technology innovator. The company

partners with regional transportation department office to build

solutions that improve traffic flow and safety. The company is

developing the following solutions:

Solution	Comments
Real Time Response	This solution will detect sudden changes in traffic flow including slow downs and stops that persist for more than one minute. The system will automatically dispatch emergency response vehicles to investigate issues. The solution will use a PySpark script to detect traffic flow changes. Script performance will be limited by available memory.
Backtrack	This solution will allow public safety officials to locate vehicles on roadways that implement traffic sensors. The solution must report changes in real time.
Planning Assistance	Transportation organizations will use Planning Assistance to analyze traffic data. The solution will allow users to define reports based on queries of the traffic data. The reports can be used for the following analyses: • current traffic load • correlation with recent local events susch as sporting events • historical traffic • tracking the travel of a single vehicle

Regional transportation departments installed traffic sensor systems on major highways across North America. Sensors record the following information each time a vehicle passes in front of a sensor:

- Time
- Location in latitude and longitude
- Speed in kilometers per second (kmps)
- License plate number
- Length of vehicle in meters

Sensors provide data by using the following structure:

```
{
    "time" : "2014-09-15T23:14:25.72511732",
    "location" : {
      "type": "Point",
      "coordinates": [
            31.9.
            -4.8
      ]
    },
    "speed": 66.2,
    "license_plate": "WA-AJ0072W",
    "vehicle_length": 4.5
}
```

Traffic sensors will occasionally capture an image of a vehicle for debugging purposes. You must optimize performance of saving/storing vehicle images.

Traffic sensor data

- Sensors must have permission only to add items to the SensorData collection.
- Traffic data insertion rate must be maximized.
- Once every three months all traffic sensor data must be analyzed to look for data patterns that indicate sensor malfunctions.
- Sensor data must be stored in a Cosmos DB named treydata in a collection named SensorData
- The impact of vehicle images on sensor data throughout must be minimized.

Backtrack

This solution reports on all data related to a specific vehicle license plate. The report must use data from the SensorData collection. Users must be able to filter vehicle data in the following ways:

- vehicles on a specific road
- vehicles driving above the speed limit

Planning Assistance

Data used for Planning Assistance must be stored in a sharded Azure SQL Database.

Data from the Sensor Data collection will automatically be loaded into the Planning Assistance database once a week by using Azure Data Factory. You must be able to manually trigger the data load process.

Privacy and security policy

- Azure Active Directory must be used for all services where it is available.
- For privacy reasons, license plate number information must not be accessible in Planning Assistance.
- Unauthorized usage of the Planning Assistance data must be detected as quickly as possible. Unauthorized usage is determined by looking for an unusual pattern of usage.
- Data must only be stored for seven years.

Performance and availability

- The report for Backtrack must execute as quickly as possible.
- The SLA for Planning Assistance is 70 percent, and multiday outages are permitted. All data must be replicated to multiple geographic regions to prevent data loss.
- You must maximize the performance of the Real Time Response system.

Financial requirements

Azure resource costs must be minimized where possible.

QUESTION 1
You need to design the runtime environment for the Real Time
Response system. What should you recommend?

A. General Purpose nodes without the Enterprise Security
   package
B. Memory Optimized Nodes without the Enterprise Security
   package
C. Memory Optimized nodes with the Enterprise Security
   package
D. General Purpose nodes with the Enterprise Security
   package

Correct Answer: B

Explanation/Reference:
Explanation:
Scenario: You must maximize the performance of the Real
Time Response system.

Testlet 2 Case study

This is a case study. Case studies are not timed separately. You can use as much exam time as you would like to complete each case. However, there may be additional case studies and sections on this exam. You must manage your time to ensure that you are able to complete all questions included on this exam in the time provided.

To answer the questions included in a case study, you will need to reference information that is provided in the case study. Case studies might contain exhibits and other resources that provide more information about the scenario that is described in the case study. Each question is independent of the other questions in this case study.

At the end of this case study, a review screen will appear. This screen allows you to review your answers and to make changes before you move to the next section of the exam. After you begin a new section, you cannot return to this section.

To start the case study
To display the first question in this case study, click the **Next** button. Use the buttons in the left pane to explore the content of the case study before you answer the questions. Clicking these buttons displays information such as business requirements, existing environment, and problem statements. If the case study has an **All Information** tab, note that the information displayed is identical to the information displayed on the subsequent tabs. When you are ready to answer a question, click the **Question** button to return to the question.

Overview

You develop data engineering solutions for Graphics Design Institute, a global media company with offices in New York City, Manchester, Singapore, and Melbourne.

The New York office hosts SQL Server databases that stores massive amounts of customer data. The company also stores millions of images on a physical server located in the New York office. More than 2 TB of image data is added each day. The images are transferred from customer devices to the server in New York.

Many images have been placed on this server in an unorganized manner, making it difficult for editors to search images. Images should automatically have object and color tags generated. The tags must be stored in a document database, and be queried by SQL.

You are hired to design a solution that can store, transform, and visualize customer data.

Requirements Business

The company identifies the following business requirements:
- You must transfer all images and customer data to cloud storage and remove on-premises servers.
- You must develop an analytical processing solution for transforming customer data.
- You must develop an image object and color tagging solution.
- Capital expenditures must be minimized.
- Cloud resource costs must be minimized.

Technical

The solution has the following technical requirements:

- Tagging data must be uploaded to the cloud from the New York office location.
- Tagging data must be replicated to regions that are geographically close to company office locations.
- Image data must be stored in a single data store at minimum cost.
- Customer data must be analyzed using managed Spark clusters.
- Power BI must be used to visualize transformed customer data.
- All data must be backed up in case disaster recovery is required.

Security and optimization

All cloud data must be encrypted at rest and in transit.
The solution must support:
- parallel processing of customer data
- hyper-scale storage of images
- global region data replication of processed image data

Testlet 3 Case study

This is a case study. Case studies are not timed separately. You can use as much exam time as you would like to complete each case. However, there may be additional case studies and sections on this exam. You must manage your time to ensure that you are able to complete all questions included on this exam in the time provided.

To answer the questions included in a case study, you will need to reference information that is provided in the case study. Case studies might contain exhibits and other resources that provide more information about the scenario that is described in the case study. Each question is independent of the other questions in this case study.

At the end of this case study, a review screen will appear. This screen allows you to review your answers and to make changes before you move to the next section of the exam. After you begin a new section, you cannot return to this section.

To start the case study
To display the first question in this case study, click the **Next** button. Use the buttons in the left pane to explore the content of the case study before you answer the questions. Clicking these buttons displays information such as business requirements, existing environment, and problem statements. If the case study has an **All Information** tab, note that the information displayed is identical to the information displayed on the subsequent tabs. When you are ready to answer a question, click the **Question** button to return to the question.

Background

Current environment

The company has the following virtual machines (VMs):

VM	Roles	Database size	VM type	Destination
CONT_SQL1	Microsoft SQL Server	2 TB	Hyper-V	Azure SQL Database
CONT_SQL2	Microsoft SQL Server	2 TB	Hyper-V	Azure SQL Database
CONT_SQL3	Microsoft SQL Server	100 GB	Hyper-V	Azure VM
CONT_SAP1	SAP	1 TB	Vmware	On-premises
CONT_SAP2	SAP	1 TB	Vmware	On-premises
CPNT_SSRS	Microsoft SQL Server Reporting Services	1 TB	Hyper-V	Azure VM

Requirements

Storage and processing

You must be able to use a file system view of data stored in a blob.
You must build an architecture that will allow Contoso to use the DB FS filesystem layer over a blob store. The architecture will need to support data files, libraries, and images. Additionally, it must provide a web-based interface to documents that contain runnable command, visualizations, and narrative text such as a notebook.

CONT_SQL3 requires an initial scale of 35000 IOPS.
CONT_SQL1 and CONT_SQL2 must use the vCore model and should include replicas. The solution must support 8000 IOPS. The storage should be configured to optimized storage for database OLTP workloads.

Migration

- You must be able to independently scale compute and storage resources.
- You must migrate all SQL Server workloads to Azure.
- You must identify related machines in the on-premises environment, get disk size data usage information. Data from SQL Server must include zone redundant storage.
- You need to ensure that app components can reside on-premises while interacting with components that run in the Azure public cloud. SAP data must remain on-premises.

- The Azure Site Recovery (ASR) results should contain per-machine data.

Business requirements

- You must design a regional disaster recovery topology.
- The database backups have regulatory purposes and must be retained for seven years.
- CONT_SQL1 stores customers sales data that requires ETL operations for data analysis. A solution is required that reads data from SQL, performs ETL, and outputs to Power BI. The solution should use managed clusters to minimize costs. To optimize logistics, Contoso needs to analyze customer sales data to see if certain products are tied to specific times in the year.
- The analytics solution for customer sales data must be available during a regional outage.

Security and auditing

- Contoso requires all corporate computers to enable
- Windows Firewall. Azure servers should be able to ping other Contoso Azure servers.
- Employee PII must be encrypted in memory, in motion, and at rest. Any data encrypted by SQL Server must support equality searches, grouping, indexing, and joining on the encrypted data.
- Keys must be secured by using hardware security modules
- (HSMs). CONT_SQL3 must not communicate over the default ports

Cost

- All solutions must minimize cost and resources.
- The organization does not want any unexpected charges.

- The data engineers must set the SQL Data Warehouse compute resources to consume 300 DWUs.
- CONT_SQL2 is not fully utilized during non-peak hours. You must minimize resource costs for during non-peak hours.

QUESTION 1
You need to optimize storage for CONT_SQL3. What should
you recommend?

A. AlwaysOn
B. Transactional processing
C. General
D. Data warehousing

Correct Answer: B

Explanation/Reference:
Explanation:
CONT_SQL3 with the SQL Server role, 100 GB database size,
Hyper-VM to be migrated to Azure VM. The storage should be
configured to optimized storage for database OLTP workloads.

Azure SQL Database provides three basic in-memory based
capabilities (built into the underlying database engine) that can
contribute in a meaningful way to performance improvements:

In-Memory Online Transactional Processing (OLTP)
Clustered columnstore indexes intended primarily for Online
Analytical Processing (OLAP) workloads Nonclustered
columnstore indexes geared towards Hybrid
Transactional/Analytical Processing (HTAP) workloads

Reference:
https://www.databasejournal.com/features/mssql/overview-of-
in-memory-technologies-of-azure-sql-database.html

Testlet 4 Case study

This is a case study. Case studies are not timed separately. You can use as much exam time as you would like to complete each case. However, there may be additional case studies and sections on this exam. You must manage your time to ensure that you are able to complete all questions included on this exam in the time provided.

To answer the questions included in a case study, you will need to reference information that is provided in the case study. Case studies might contain exhibits and other resources that provide more information about the scenario that is described in the case study. Each question is independent of the other questions in this case study.

At the end of this case study, a review screen will appear. This screen allows you to review your answers and to make changes before you move to the next section of the exam. After you begin a new section, you cannot return to this section.

To start the case study
To display the first question in this case study, click the **Next** button. Use the buttons in the left pane to explore the content of the case study before you answer the questions. Clicking these buttons displays information such as business requirements, existing environment, and problem statements. If the case study has an **All Information** tab, note that the information displayed is identical to the information displayed on the subsequent tabs. When you are ready to answer a question, click the **Question** button to return to the question.

Overview General Overview

ADatum Corporation is a medical company that has 5,000 physicians located in more than 300 hospitals across the US. The company has a medical department, a sales department, a marketing department, a medical research department, and a human resources department.

You are redesigning the application environment of ADatum.

Physical Locations

ADatum has three main offices in New York, Dallas, and Los Angeles. The offices connect to each other by using a WAN link. Each office connects directly to the Internet. The Los Angeles office also has a datacenter that hosts all the company's applications.

Existing Environment Health Review

ADatum has a critical OLTP web application named Health Review that physicians use to track billing, patient care, and overall physician best practices.

Health Interface

ADatum has a critical application named Health Interface that receives hospital messages related to patient care and status updates. The messages are sent in batches by each hospital's enterprise relationship management (ERM) system by using a VPN. The data sent from each hospital can have varying columns and formats.

Currently, a custom C# application is used to send the data to Health Interface. The application uses deprecated libraries and a new solution must be designed for this functionality.

Health Insights

ADatum has a web-based reporting system named Health Insights that shows hospital and patient insights to physicians and business users. The data is created from the data in Health Review and Health Interface, as well as manual entries.

Database Platform

Currently, the databases for all three applications are hosted on an out-of-date VMware cluster that has a single instance of Microsoft SQL Server 2012.

Problem Statements

ADatum identifies the following issues in its current environment:

- Over time, the data received by Health Interface from the hospitals has slowed, and the number of messages has increased. When a new hospital joins ADatum, Health Interface requires a schema modification due to the lack of data standardization. The speed of batch data processing is inconsistent.

Business Requirements Business Goals

ADatum identifies the following business goals:

- Migrate the applications to Azure whenever possible.
- Minimize the development effort required to perform data movement.
- Provide continuous integration and deployment for development, test, and production environments.
- Provide faster access to the applications and the data and provide more consistent application performance.
- Minimize the number of services required to perform data processing, development, scheduling, monitoring, and the operationalizing of pipelines.

Health Review Requirements

ADatum identifies the following requirements for the Health Review application:
- Ensure that sensitive health data is encrypted at rest and in transit.

- Tag all the sensitive health data in Health Review. The data will be used for auditing.

Health Interface Requirements

ADatum identifies the following requirements for the Health Interface application:

- Upgrade to a data storage solution that will provide flexible schemas and increased throughput for writing data. Data must be regionally located close to each hospital, and reads must display be the most recent committed version of an item.
- Reduce the amount of time it takes to add data from new
- hospitals to Health Interface. Support a more scalable batch

processing solution in Azure.
- Reduce the amount of development effort to rewrite existing SQL queries.

Health Insights Requirements

ADatum identifies the following requirements for the Health Insights application:

- The analysis of events must be performed over time by using an organizational date dimension table.
- The data from Health Interface and Health Review must be available in Health Insights within 15 minutes of being committed.
- The new Health Insights application must be built on a massively parallel processing (MPP) architecture that will support the high performance of joins on large fact tables.

QUESTION 1
What should you recommend as a batch processing solution for Health Interface?

A. Azure CycleCloud
B. Azure Stream Analytics
C. Azure Data Factory
D. Azure Databricks

Correct Answer: B

Explanation/Reference:
Explanation:
Scenario: ADatum identifies the following requirements for the Health Interface application:
Support a more scalable batch processing solution in Azure.
Reduce the amount of time it takes to add data from new hospitals to Health Interface.

Data Factory integrates with the Azure Cosmos DB bulk executor library to provide the best performance when you write to Azure Cosmos DB.

Reference:
https://docs.microsoft.com/en-us/azure/data-factory/connector-azure-cosmos-db

Testlet 5 Overview

You are a data engineer for Trey Research. The company is close to completing a joint project with the government to build smart highways infrastructure across North America. This involves the placement of sensors and cameras to measure traffic flow, car speed, and vehicle details.

You have been asked to design a cloud solution that will meet the business and technical requirements of the smart highway.

Solution components Telemetry Capture

The telemetry capture system records each time a vehicle passes in front of a sensor. The sensors run on a custom embedded operating system and record the following telemetry data:

- Time
- Location in latitude and longitude
- 1Speed in kilometers per hour (kmph)
- Length of vehicle in meters

Visual Monitoring

The visual monitoring system is a network of approximately 1,000 cameras placed near highways that capture images of vehicle traffic every 2 seconds. The cameras record high resolution images. Each image is approximately 3 MB in size.

Requirements. Business

The company identifies the following business requirements:

- External vendors must be able to perform custom analysis of data using machine learning technologies.
- You must display a dashboard on the operations status page that displays the following metrics: telemetry, volume, and processing latency.
- Traffic data must be made available to the Government Planning Department for the purpose of modeling changes to the highway system. The traffic data will be used in
- conjunction with other data such as information about events such as sporting events, weather conditions, and population statistics. External data used during the modeling

is stored in on-premises SQL Server 2016 databases and CSV files stored in an Azure Data Lake Storage Gen2 storage account. Information about vehicles that have been detected as going over the speed limit during the last 30 minutes must be available to law enforcement officers. Several law enforcement organizations may respond to speeding vehicles.

- The solution must allow for searches of vehicle images by license plate to support law enforcement investigations. Searches must be able to be performed using a query language and must support fuzzy searches to compensate for license plate detection errors.

Requirements. Security

The solution must meet the following security requirements:

- External vendors must not have direct access to sensor data or images.
- Images produced by the vehicle monitoring solution must be deleted after one month. You must minimize costs associated with deleting images from the data store.
- Unauthorized usage of data must be detected in real time. Unauthorized usage is determined by looking for unusual usage patterns.
- All changes to Azure resources used by the solution must be recorded and stored. Data must be provided to the security team for incident response purposes.

Requirements. Sensor data

You must write all telemetry data to the closest Azure region. The sensors used for the telemetry capture system have a small amount of memory available and so must write data as quickly as possible to avoid losing telemetry data.

Testlet 6 Case study

This is a case study. Case studies are not timed separately. You can use as much exam time as you would like to complete each case. However, there may be additional case studies and sections on this exam. You must manage your time to ensure that you are able to complete all questions included on this exam in the time provided.

To answer the questions included in a case study, you will need to reference information that is provided in the case study. Case studies might contain exhibits and other resources that provide more information about the scenario that is described in the case study. Each question is independent of the other questions in this case study.

At the end of this case study, a review screen will appear. This screen allows you to review your answers and to make changes before you move to the next section of the exam. After you begin a new section, you cannot return to this section.

To start the case study
To display the first question in this case study, click the **Next** button. Use the buttons in the left pane to explore the content of the case study before you answer the questions. Clicking these buttons displays information such as business requirements, existing environment, and problem statements. If the case study has an **All Information** tab, note that the information displayed is identical to the information displayed on the subsequent tabs. When you are ready to answer a question, click the **Question** button to return to the question.

Overview

Litware, Inc. owns and operates 300 convenience stores across the US. The company sells a variety of packaged foods and drinks, as well as a variety of prepared foods, such as sandwiches and pizzas.

Litware has a loyalty club whereby members can get daily discounts on specific items by providing their membership number at checkout.

Litware employs business analysts who prefer to analyze data by using Microsoft Power BI, and data scientists who prefer

analyzing data in Azure Databricks notebooks.

Requirements. Business Goals

Litware wants to create a new analytics environment in Azure to meet the following requirements:

- See inventory levels across the stores.
- Data must be updated as close to real time as possible.
- Execute ad hoc analytical queries on historical data to identify whether the loyalty club discounts increase sales of the discounted products.
- Every four hours, notify store employees about how many prepared food items to produce based on historical demand from the sales data.

Requirements. Technical Requirements

Litware identifies the following technical requirements:

- Minimize the number of different Azure services needed to achieve the business goals
- Use platform as a service (PaaS) offerings whenever possible and avoid having to provision virtual machines that must be managed by Litware.
- Ensure that the analytical data store is accessible only to the company's on-premises network and Azure services.
- Use Azure Active Directory (Azure AD) authentication whenever possible. Use the principle of least privilege when designing security.
- Stage inventory data in Azure Data Lake Storage Gen2 before loading the data into the analytical data store.
- Litware wants to remove transient data from Data Lake Storage once the data is no longer in use. Files that have a modified date that is older than 14 days must be removed.
- Limit the business analysts' access to customer contact information, such as phone numbers, because this type of data is not analytically relevant.
- Ensure that you can quickly restore a copy of the analytical data store within one hour in the event of corruption or accidental deletion.

Requirements. Planned Environment

Litware plans to implement the following environment:

- The application development team will create an Azure event hub to receive real-time sales data, including store number, date, time, product ID, customer loyalty number, price, and discount amount, from the point of sale (POS) system and output the data to data storage in Azure.
- Customer data, including name, contact information, and loyalty number, comes from Salesforce and can be imported into Azure once every eight hours. Row modified dates are not trusted in the source table.
- Product data, including product ID, name, and category, comes from Salesforce and can be imported into Azure once every eight hours. Row modified dates are not trusted in the source table.
- Daily inventory data comes from a Microsoft SQL server located on a private network.
- Litware currently has 5 TB of historical sales data and 100 GB of customer data. The company expects approximately 100 GB of new data per month for the next year.
- Litware will build a custom application named FoodPrep to provide store employees with the calculation results of how many prepared food items to produce every four hours.
- Litware does not plan to implement Azure ExpressRoute or a VPN between the on-premises network and Azure.

QUESTION 1

Inventory levels must be calculated by subtracting the current day's sales from the previous day's final inventory.

Which two options provide Litware with the ability to quickly calculate the current inventory levels by store and product? Each correct answer presents a complete solution.

NOTE: Each correct selection is worth one point.

A. Consume the output of the event hub by using Azure Stream Analytics and aggregate the data by store and product. Output the resulting data directly to Azure Synapse Analytics. Use Transact-SQL to calculate the inventory levels.

B. Output Event Hubs Avro files to Azure Blob storage. Use Transact-SQL to calculate the inventory levels by using PolyBase in Azure Synapse Analytics.

C. Consume the output of the event hub by using Databricks. Use Databricks to calculate the inventory levels and output the data to Azure Synapse Analytics.

D. Consume the output of the event hub by using Azure Stream Analytics and aggregate the data by store and product. Output the resulting data into Databricks. Calculate the inventory levels in Databricks and output the data to Azure Blob storage.

E. Output Event Hubs Avro files to Azure Blob storage. Trigger an Azure Data Factory copy activity to run every 10 minutes to load the data into Azure Synapse Analytics. Use Transact-SQL to aggregate the data by store and product.

Correct Answer: AE

Explanation/Reference:
Explanation:
A: Azure Stream Analytics is a fully managed service providing low-latency, highly available, scalable complex event processing over streaming data in the cloud. You can use your Azure SQL Data Warehouse database as an output sink for your Stream Analytics jobs.

E: Event Hubs Capture is the easiest way to get data into Azure. Using Azure Data Lake, Azure Data Factory, and Azure

HDInsight, you can perform batch processing and other analytics using familiar tools and platforms of your choosing, at any scale you need.

Note: Event Hubs Capture creates files in Avro format.

Captured data is written in Apache Avro format: a compact, fast, binary format that provides rich data structures with inline schema. This format is widely used in the Hadoop ecosystem, Stream Analytics, and Azure Data Factory.

Scenario: The application development team will create an Azure event hub to receive real-time sales data, including store number, date, time, product ID, customer loyalty number, price, and discount amount, from the point of sale (POS) system and output the data to data storage in Azure.

Reference:
https://docs.microsoft.com/bs-latn-ba/azure/sql-data-warehouse/sql-data-warehouse-integrate-azure-stream-analytics https://docs.microsoft.com/en-us/azure/event-hubs/event-hubs-capture-overview

QUESTION 1

You are designing an enterprise data warehouse in Azure Synapse Analytics. You plan to load millions of rows of data into the data warehouse each day. You must ensure that staging tables are optimized for data loading.
You need to design the staging tables.

What type of tables should you recommend?

A. Round-robin distributed table
B. Hash-distributed table
C. Replicated table
D. External table

Correct Answer: A

Explanation/Reference:
Explanation:
To achieve the fastest loading speed for moving data into a data warehouse table, load data into a staging table. Define the staging table as a heap and use round- robin for the distribution option.

Incorrect:
Not B: Consider that loading is usually a two-step process in which you first load to a staging table and then insert the data into a production data warehouse table. If the production table uses a hash distribution, the total time to load and insert might be faster if you define the staging table with the hash distribution. Loading to the staging table takes longer, but the second step of inserting the rows to the production table does not incur data movement across the distributions.

Reference:
https://docs.microsoft.com/en-us/azure/sql-data-warehouse/guidance-for-loading-data

QUESTION 2
A company has an application that uses Azure SQL Database as the data store.

The application experiences a large increase in activity during the last month of each year.

You need to manually scale the Azure SQL Database instance to account for the increase in data write operations. Which scaling method should you recommend?

A. Scale up by using elastic pools to distribute resources.
B. Scale out by sharding the data across databases.
C. Scale up by increasing the database throughput units.

Correct Answer: C

Explanation/Reference:
Explanation:
As of now, the cost of running an Azure SQL database instance is based on the number of Database Throughput Units (DTUs) allocated for the database. When determining the number of units to allocate for the solution, a major contributing factor is to identify what processing power is needed to handle the volume of expected requests.
Running the statement to upgrade/downgrade your database takes a matter of seconds.

Incorrect Answers:
A: Elastic pools is used if there are two or more databases.

Reference:
https://www.skylinetechnologies.com/Blog/Skyline-Blog/August_2017/dynamically-scale-azure-sql-database

QUESTION 3

You are designing an Azure Data Factory pipeline for processing data. The pipeline will process data that is stored in general-purpose standard Azure storage. You need to ensure that the compute environment is created on-demand and removed when the process is completed.

Which type of activity should you recommend?

A. Databricks Python activity
B. Data Lake Analytics U-SQL activity
C. HDInsight Pig activity
D. Databricks Jar activity

Correct Answer: C

Explanation/Reference:
Explanation:

The HDInsight Pig activity in a Data Factory pipeline executes Pig queries on your own or on-demand HDInsight cluster.

Reference:
https://docs.microsoft.com/en-us/azure/data-factory/transform-data-using-hadoop-pig

QUESTION 4
A company installs IoT devices to monitor its fleet of delivery vehicles. Data from devices is collected from Azure Event Hub. The data must be transmitted to Power BI for real-time data visualizations.

You need to recommend a solution. What should you recommend?

A. Azure HDInsight with Spark Streaming
B. Apache Spark in Azure Databricks
C. Azure Stream Analytics
D. Azure HDInsight with Storm

Correct Answer: C

Explanation/Reference:
Explanation:
Step 1: Get your IoT hub ready for data access by adding a consumer group.
Step 2: Create, configure, and run a Stream Analytics job for data transfer from your IoT hub to your Power BI account. Step 3: Create and publish a Power BI report to visualize the data.

Reference:
https://docs.microsoft.com/en-us/azure/iot-hub/iot-hub-live-data-visualization-in-power-bi

QUESTION 5

You have a Windows-based solution that analyzes scientific data. You are designing a cloud-based solution that performs real-time analysis of the data. You need to design the logical flow for the solution.

Which two actions should you recommend? Each correct answer presents part of the solution.

NOTE: Each correct selection is worth one point.

A. Send data from the application to an Azure Stream Analytics job.

B. Use an Azure Stream Analytics job on an edge device. Ingress data from an Azure Data Factory instance and build queries that output to Power BI.

C. Use an Azure Stream Analytics job in the cloud. Ingress data from the Azure Event Hub instance and build queries that output to Power BI.

D. Use an Azure Stream Analytics job in the cloud. Ingress data from an Azure Event Hub instance and build queries that output to Azure Data Lake Storage.

E. Send data from the application to Azure Data Lake Storage.

F. Send data from the application to an Azure Event Hub instance.

Correct Answer: CF

Explanation/Reference:
Explanation:
Stream Analytics has first-class integration with Azure data streams as inputs from three kinds of resources:
- Azure Event Hubs
- Azure IoT Hub Azure Blob storage

Reference:
https://docs.microsoft.com/en-us/azure/stream-analytics/stream-analytics-define-inputs

QUESTION 6
You are designing a real-time stream solution based on Azure
Functions. The solution will process data uploaded to Azure
Blob Storage. The solution requirements are as follows:

- New blobs must be processed with a little delay as possible.
- Scaling must occur automatically.
- Costs must be minimized. What should you recommend?

A. Deploy the Azure Function in an App Service plan and use
a Blob trigger.

B. Deploy the Azure Function in a Consumption plan and use
an Event Grid trigger.

C. Deploy the Azure Function in a Consumption plan and use a
Blob trigger.

D. Deploy the Azure Function in an App Service plan and use
an Event Grid trigger.

Correct Answer: C

Explanation/Reference:
Explanation:
Create a function, with the help of a blob trigger template, which
is triggered when files are uploaded to or updated in Azure Blob
storage.
You use a consumption plan, which is a hosting plan that
defines how resources are allocated to your function app. In the
default Consumption Plan, resources are added dynamically as
required by your functions. In this serverless hosting, you only
pay for the time your functions run. When you run in an App
Service plan, you must manage the scaling of your function
app.

Reference:
https://docs.microsoft.com/en-us/azure/azure-
functions/functions-create-storage-blob-triggered-function

QUESTION 7
You plan to migrate data to Azure SQL Database.

The database must remain synchronized with updates to
Microsoft Azure and SQL Server. You need to set up the
database as a subscriber.

What should you recommend?

A. Azure Data Factory
B. SQL Server Data Tools
C. Data Migration Assistant
D. SQL Server Agent for SQL Server 2017 or later
E. SQL Server Management Studio 17.9.1 or later

Correct Answer: E

Explanation/Reference:
Explanation:
To set up the database as a subscriber we need to configure
database replication. You can use SQL Server Management
Studio to configure replication. Use the latest versions of SQL
Server Management Studio in order to be able to use all the
features of Azure SQL Database.

Reference:
https://www.sqlshack.com/sql-server-database-migration-to-
azure-sql-database-using-sql-server-transactional-replication/

QUESTION 8
You design data engineering solutions for a company.

A project requires analytics and visualization of large set of data. The project has the following requirements:

- Notebook scheduling
- Cluster automation
- Power BI Visualization

You need to recommend the appropriate Azure service. Which Azure service should you recommend?

A. Azure Batch
B. Azure Stream Analytics
C. Azure ML Studio
D. Azure Databricks
E. Azure HDInsight

Correct Answer: D

Explanation/Reference:
Explanation:
A databrick job is a way of running a notebook or JAR either immediately or on a scheduled basis.

Azure Databricks has two types of clusters: interactive and job. Interactive clusters are used to analyze data collaboratively with interactive notebooks. Job clusters are used to run fast and robust automated workloads using the UI or API.

You can visualize Data with Azure Databricks and Power BI Desktop.

Reference:
https://docs.azuredatabricks.net/user-guide/clusters/index.html
https://docs.azuredatabricks.net/user-guide/jobs.html

QUESTION 9
A company plans to use Apache Spark Analytics to analyze intrusion detection data.

You need to recommend a solution to monitor network and system activities for malicious activities and policy violations. Reports must be produced in an electronic format and sent to management. The solution must minimize administrative efforts.

What should you recommend?

A. Azure Data Factory
B. Azure Data Lake
C. Azure Databricks
D. Azure HDInsight

Correct Answer: D

Explanation/Reference:
Explanation:
With Azure HDInsight you can set up Azure Monitor alerts that will trigger when the value of a metric or the results of a query meet certain conditions. You can condition on a query returning a record with a value that is greater than or less than a certain threshold, or even on the number of results returned by a query. For example, you could create an alert to send an email if a Spark job fails or if a Kafka disk usage becomes over 90 percent full.

Reference:
https://azure.microsoft.com/en-us/blog/monitoring-on-azure-hdinsight-part-4-workload-metrics-and-logs/

QUESTION 10
You are designing an Azure Databricks interactive cluster. The cluster will be used infrequently and will be configured for auto-termination. You need to ensure that the cluster configuration is retained indefinitely after the cluster is terminated. The solution must minimize costs. What should you do?

A. Clone the cluster after it is terminated.
B. Terminate the cluster manually when processing completes.
C. Create an Azure runbook that starts the cluster every 90 days.
D. Pin the cluster.

Correct Answer: D

Explanation/Reference:
Explanation:
To keep an interactive cluster configuration even after it has been terminated for more than 30 days, an administrator can pin a cluster to the cluster list.

Reference:
https://docs.azuredatabricks.net/clusters/clusters-manage.html#automatic-termination

QUESTION 11

You need to design a telemetry data solution that supports the analysis of log files in real time.

Which two Azure services should you include in the solution? Each correct answer presents part of the solution.

NOTE: Each correct selection is worth one point.

A. Azure Databricks
B. Azure Data Factory
C. Azure Event Hubs
D. Azure Data Lake Storage Gen2
E. Azure IoT Hub

Correct Answer: AC

Explanation/Reference:
Explanation:
You connect a data ingestion system with Azure Databricks to stream data into an Apache Spark cluster in near real-time. You set up data ingestion system using Azure Event Hubs and then connect it to Azure Databricks to process the messages coming through.

Note: Azure Event Hubs is a highly scalable data streaming platform and event ingestion service, capable of receiving and processing millions of events per second. Event Hubs can process and store events, data, or telemetry produced by distributed software and devices. Data sent to an event hub can be transformed and stored using any real-time analytics provider or batching/storage adapters.

Reference:
https://docs.microsoft.com/en-us/azure/azure-databricks/databricks-stream-from-eventhubs

QUESTION 12

You are planning a design pattern based on the Lambda
architecture as shown in the exhibit.

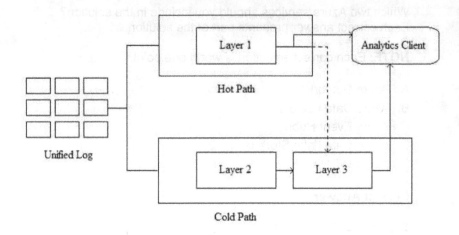

Which Azure service should you use for the hot path?

A. Azure Databricks
B. Azure SQL Database
C. Azure Data Factory
D. Azure Database for PostgreSQL

Correct Answer: A

Explanation/Reference:
Explanation:
In Azure, all of the following data stores will meet the core
requirements supporting real-time processing:

- Apache Spark in Azure Databricks
- Azure Stream Analytics
- HDInsight with Spark Streaming
- HDInsight with Storm

- Azure Functions
- Azure App Service WebJobs

Note: Lambda architectures use batch-processing, stream-processing, and a serving layer to minimize the latency involved in querying big data.

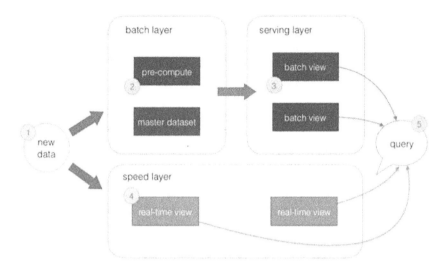

Reference:

https://azure.microsoft.com/en-us/blog/lambda-architecture-using-azure-cosmosdb-faster-performance-low-tco-low-devops/
https://docs.microsoft.com/en-us/azure/architecture/data-guide/technology-choices/stream-processing

QUESTION 13

You are designing an audit strategy for an Azure SQL Database environment.

You need to recommend a solution to provide real-time notifications for potential security breaches. The solution must minimize development effort. Which destination should you include in the recommendation?

A. Azure Blob storage
B. Azure SQL Data Warehouse
C. Azure Event Hubs
D. Azure Log Analytics

Correct Answer: D

Explanation/Reference:
Explanation:
Auditing for Azure SQL Database and SQL Data Warehouse tracks database events and writes them to an audit log in your Azure storage account, Log Analytics workspace or Event Hubs.

Alerts in Azure Monitor can identify important information in your Log Analytics repository. They are created by alert rules that automatically run log searches at regular intervals, and if results of the log search match particular criteria, then an alert record is created and it can be configured to perform an automated response.

Reference:
https://docs.microsoft.com/en-us/azure/sql-database/sql-database-auditing https://docs.microsoft.com/en-us/azure/azure-monitor/learn/tutorial-response

QUESTION 14

You need to design a real-time stream solution that uses Azure Functions to process data uploaded to Azure Blob Storage. The solution must meet the following requirements:

- Support up to 1 million blobs.
- Scaling must occur automatically.
- Costs must be minimized.

What should you recommend?

A. Deploy the Azure Function in an App Service plan and use a Blob trigger.

B. Deploy the Azure Function in a Consumption plan and use an Event Grid trigger.

C. Deploy the Azure Function in a Consumption plan and use a Blob trigger.

D. Deploy the Azure Function in an App Service plan and use an Event Grid trigger.

Correct Answer: C

Explanation/Reference:
Explanation:
Create a function, with the help of a blob trigger template, which is triggered when files are uploaded to or updated in Azure Blob storage.
You use a consumption plan, which is a hosting plan that defines how resources are allocated to your function app. In the default Consumption Plan, resources are added dynamically as required by your functions. In this serverless hosting, you only pay for the time your functions run. When you run in an App Service plan, you must manage the scaling of your function app.

Reference:
https://docs.microsoft.com/en-us/azure/azure-functions/functions-create-storage-blob-triggered-function

QUESTION 15

A company purchases IoT devices to monitor manufacturing machinery. The company uses an IoT appliance to communicate with the IoT devices. The company must be able to monitor the devices in real-time.

You need to design the solution. What should you recommend?

A. Azure Data Factory instance using Azure PowerShell
B. Azure Analysis Services using Microsoft Visual Studio
C. Azure Stream Analytics cloud job using Azure PowerShell
D. Azure Data Factory instance using Microsoft Visual Studio

Correct Answer: C

Explanation/Reference:
Explanation:
Stream Analytics is a cost-effective event processing engine that helps uncover real-time insights from devices, sensors, infrastructure, applications and data quickly and easily.

Monitor and manage Stream Analytics resources with Azure PowerShell cmdlets and powershell scripting that execute basic Stream Analytics tasks.

Reference:
https://cloudblogs.microsoft.com/sqlserver/2014/10/29/microsoft -adds-iot-streaming-analytics-data-production-and-workflow- services-to-azure/

QUESTION 16

A company purchases IoT devices to monitor manufacturing machinery. The company uses an IoT appliance to communicate with the IoT devices. The company must be able to monitor the devices in real-time.

You need to design the solution. What should you recommend?

A. Azure Data Factory instance using Azure PowerShell
B. Azure Analysis Services using Microsoft Visual Studio
C. Azure Stream Analytics Edge application using Microsoft Visual Studio
D. Azure Analysis Services using Azure PowerShell

Correct Answer: C

Explanation/Reference:
Explanation:
Azure Stream Analytics (ASA) on IoT Edge empowers developers to deploy near-real-time analytical intelligence closer to IoT devices so that they can unlock the full value of device-generated data.

References:
https://docs.microsoft.com/en-us/azure/stream-analytics/stream-analytics-edge

QUESTION 17
You plan to ingest streaming social media data by using Azure Stream Analytics. The data will be stored in files in Azure Data Lake Storage, and then consumed by using Azure Databricks and PolyBase in Azure SQL Data Warehouse.

You need to recommend a Stream Analytics data output format to ensure that the queries from Databricks and PolyBase against the files encounter the fewest possible errors. The solution must ensure that the files can be queried quickly and that the data type information is retained.

What should you recommend?

A. Avro
B. CSV
C. Parquet
D. JSON

Correct Answer: A

Explanation/Reference:
Explanation:
The Avro format is great for data and message preservation.

Avro schema with its support for evolution is essential for making the data robust for streaming architectures like Kafka, and with the metadata that schema provides, you can reason on the data. Having a schema provides robustness in providing meta-data about the data stored in Avro records which are self-documenting the data.

References: http://cloudurable.com/blog/avro/index.html

Testlet 1 Case study

This is a case study. Case studies are not timed separately. You can use as much exam time as you would like to complete each case. However, there may be additional case studies and sections on this exam. You must manage your time to ensure that you are able to complete all questions included on this exam in the time provided.

To answer the questions included in a case study, you will need to reference information that is provided in the case study. Case studies might contain exhibits and other resources that provide more information about the scenario that is described in the case study. Each question is independent of the other questions in this case study.

At the end of this case study, a review screen will appear. This screen allows you to review your answers and to make changes before you move to the next section of the exam. After you begin a new section, you cannot return to this section.

To start the case study
To display the first question in this case study, click the **Next** button. Use the buttons in the left pane to explore the content of the case study before you answer the questions. Clicking these buttons displays information such as business requirements, existing environment, and problem statements. If the case study has an **All Information** tab, note that the information displayed is identical to the information displayed on the subsequent tabs. When you are ready to answer a question, click the **Question** button to return to the question.

Overview

Litware, Inc. owns and operates 300 convenience stores across the US. The company sells a variety of packaged foods and drinks, as well as a variety of prepared foods, such as sandwiches and pizzas.

Litware has a loyalty club whereby members can get daily discounts on specific items by providing their membership number at checkout.

Litware employs business analysts who prefer to analyze data by using Microsoft Power BI, and data scientists who prefer

analyzing data in Azure Databricks notebooks.

Requirements. Business Goals
Litware wants to create a new analytics environment in Azure to meet the following requirements:

- See inventory levels across the stores.
- Data must be updated as close to real time as possible.
- Execute ad hoc analytical queries on historical data to identify whether the loyalty club discounts increase sales of the discounted products.
- Every four hours, notify store employees about how many prepared food items to produce based on historical demand from the sales data.

Requirements. Technical Requirements

Litware identifies the following technical requirements:

- Minimize the number of different Azure services needed to achieve the business goals
- Use platform as a service (PaaS) offerings whenever possible and avoid having to provision virtual machines that must be managed by Litware.
- Ensure that the analytical data store is accessible only to the company's on-premises network and Azure services.
- Use Azure Active Directory (Azure AD) authentication whenever possible.
- Use the principle of least privilege when designing security.
- Stage inventory data in Azure Data Lake Storage Gen2 before loading the data into the analytical data store.
- Litware wants to remove transient data from Data Lake Storage once the data is no longer in use. Files that have a modified date that is older than 14 days must be removed.
- Limit the business analysts' access to customer contact information, such as phone numbers, because this type of data is not analytically relevant.
- Ensure that you can quickly restore a copy of the analytical data store within one hour in the event of corruption or accidental deletion.

Requirements. Planned Environment

Litware plans to implement the following environment:
- The application development team will create an Azure event hub to receive real-time sales data, including store number, date, time, product ID, customer loyalty number,

price, and discount amount, from the point of sale (POS) system and output the data to data storage in Azure.

- Customer data, including name, contact information, and loyalty number, comes from Salesforce and can be imported into Azure once every eight hours. Row modified dates are not trusted in the source table.
- Product data, including product ID, name, and category, comes from Salesforce and can be imported into Azure once every eight hours. Row modified dates are not trusted in the source table.
- Daily inventory data comes from a Microsoft SQL server located on a private network.
- Litware currently has 5 TB of historical sales data and 100 GB of customer data. The company expects approximately 100 GB of new data per month for the next year.
- Litware will build a custom application named FoodPrep to provide store employees with the calculation results of how many prepared food items to produce every four hours.
- Litware does not plan to implement Azure ExpressRoute or a VPN between the on-premises network and Azure.

QUESTION 1

What should you recommend to prevent users outside the Litware on-premises network from accessing the analytical data store?

A. a server-level virtual network rule

B. a database-level virtual network rule

C. a database-level firewall IP rule

D. a server-level firewall IP rule

Correct Answer: A

Explanation/Reference:
Explanation:

Scenario: Ensure that the analytical data store is accessible only to the company's on-premises network and Azure services.

Virtual network rules are one firewall security feature that controls whether the database server for your single databases and elastic pool in Azure SQL Database or for your databases in SQL Data Warehouse accepts communications that are sent from particular subnets in virtual networks.

Server-level, not database-level: Each virtual network rule applies to your whole Azure SQL Database server, not just to one particular database on the server. In other words, virtual network rule applies at the server-level, not at the database-level.

Reference:
https://docs.microsoft.com/en-us/azure/sql-database/sql-database-vnet-service-endpoint-rule-overview

QUESTION 2
What should you recommend using to secure sensitive customer contact information?

A. data labels
B. column-level security
C. row-level security
D. Transparent Data Encryption (TDE)

Correct Answer: B

Explanation/Reference:
Explanation:
Scenario: Limit the business analysts' access to customer contact information, such as phone numbers, because this type of data is not analytically relevant.

Always Encrypted is a feature designed to protect sensitive data stored in specific database columns from access (for example, credit card numbers, national identification numbers, or data on a need to know basis). This includes database administrators or other privileged users who are authorized to access the database to perform management tasks, but have no business need to access the particular data in the encrypted columns. The data is always encrypted, which means the encrypted data is decrypted only for processing by client applications with access to the encryption key.

Incorrect Answers:
A: Transparent Data Encryption (TDE) encrypts SQL Server, Azure SQL Database, and Azure SQL Data Warehouse data files, known as encrypting data at rest. TDE does not provide encryption across communication channels.

Reference:
https://docs.microsoft.com/en-us/azure/sql-database/sql-database-security-overview

Testlet 2 Case study

This is a case study. Case studies are not timed separately. You can use as much exam time as you would like to complete each case. However, there may be additional case studies and sections on this exam. You must manage your time to ensure that you are able to complete all questions included on this exam in the time provided.

To answer the questions included in a case study, you will need to reference information that is provided in the case study. Case studies might contain exhibits and other resources that provide more information about the scenario that is described in the case study. Each question is independent of the other questions in this case study.

At the end of this case study, a review screen will appear. This screen allows you to review your answers and to make changes before you move to the next section of the exam. After you begin a new section, you cannot return to this section.

To start the case study
To display the first question in this case study, click the **Next** button. Use the buttons in the left pane to explore the content of the case study before you answer the questions. Clicking these buttons displays information such as business requirements, existing environment, and problem statements. If the case study has an **All Information** tab, note that the information displayed is identical to the information displayed on the subsequent tabs. When you are ready to answer a question, click the **Question** button to return to the question.

Background

Current environment

The company has the following virtual machines (VMs):

VM	Roles	Database size	VM type	Destination
CONT_SQL1	Microsoft SQL Server	2 TB	Hyper-V	Azure SQL Database
CONT_SQL2	Microsoft SQL Server	2 TB	Hyper-V	Azure SQL Database
CONT_SQL3	Microsoft SQL Server	100 GB	Hyper-V	Azure VM
CONT_SAP1	SAP	1 TB	Vmware	On-premises
CONT_SAP2	SAP	1 TB	Vmware	On-premises
CPNT_SSRS	Microsoft SQL Server Reporting Services	1 TB	Hyper-V	Azure VM

Requirements

Storage and processing

You must be able to use a file system view of data stored in a blob.
You must build an architecture that will allow Contoso to use the DB FS filesystem layer over a blob store. The architecture will need to support data files, libraries, and images.
Additionally, it must provide a web-based interface to documents that contain runnable command, visualizations, and narrative text such as a notebook.

CONT_SQL3 requires an initial scale of 35000 IOPS.
CONT_SQL1 and CONT_SQL2 must use the vCore model and should include replicas. The solution must support 8000 IOPS. The storage should be configured to optimized storage for database OLTP workloads.

Migration
- You must be able to independently scale compute and storage resources.
- You must migrate all SQL Server workloads to Azure.
- You must identify related machines in the on-premises environment, get disk size data usage information.
- Data from SQL Server must include zone redundant storage.
- You need to ensure that app components can reside on-premises while interacting with components that run in the Azure public cloud.
- SAP data must remain on-premises.
- The Azure Site Recovery (ASR) results should contain per-machine data.

Business requirements

- You must design a regional disaster recovery topology.
- The database backups have regulatory purposes and must be retained for seven years.
- CONT_SQL1 stores customers sales data that requires ETL operations for data analysis. A solution is required that reads data from SQL, performs ETL, and outputs to Power BI. The solution should use managed clusters to minimize costs. To optimize logistics, Contoso needs to analyze customer sales data to see if certain products are tied to specific times in the year.
- The analytics solution for customer sales data must be available during a regional outage.

Security and auditing

- Contoso requires all corporate computers to enable
- Windows Firewall. Azure servers should be able to ping other Contoso Azure servers.
- Employee PII must be encrypted in memory, in motion, and at rest. Any data encrypted by SQL Server must support equality searches, grouping, indexing, and joining on the encrypted data.
- Keys must be secured by using hardware security modules (HSMs). CONT_SQL3 must not communicate over the default ports

Cost

- All solutions must minimize cost and resources.
- The organization does not want any unexpected charges.
- The data engineers must set the SQL Data Warehouse compute resources to consume 300 DWUs.
- CONT_SQL2 is not fully utilized during non-peak hours. You must minimize resource costs for during non-peak hours.

Testlet 3 Case study

This is a case study. Case studies are not timed separately. You can use as much exam time as you would like to complete each case. However, there may be additional case studies and sections on this exam. You must manage your time to ensure that you are able to complete all questions included on this exam in the time provided.

To answer the questions included in a case study, you will need to reference information that is provided in the case study. Case studies might contain exhibits and other resources that provide more information about the scenario that is described in the case study. Each question is independent of the other questions in this case study.

At the end of this case study, a review screen will appear. This screen allows you to review your answers and to make changes before you move to the next section of the exam. After you begin a new section, you cannot return to this section.

To start the case study
To display the first question in this case study, click the **Next** button. Use the buttons in the left pane to explore the content of the case study before you answer the questions. Clicking these buttons displays information such as business requirements, existing environment, and problem statements. If the case study has an **All Information** tab, note that the information displayed is identical to the information displayed on the subsequent tabs. When you are ready to answer a question, click the **Question** button to return to the question.

Overview General Overview

ADatum Corporation is a medical company that has 5,000 physicians located in more than 300 hospitals across the US. The company has a medical department, a sales department, a marketing department, a medical research department, and a human resources department.

You are redesigning the application environment of ADatum.

Physical Locations

ADatum has three main offices in New York, Dallas, and Los

Angeles. The offices connect to each other by using a WAN link. Each office connects directly to the Internet. The Los Angeles office also has a datacenter that hosts all the company's applications.

Existing Environment Health Review

ADatum has a critical OLTP web application named Health Review that physicians use to track billing, patient care, and overall physician best practices.

Health Interface

ADatum has a critical application named Health Interface that receives hospital messages related to patient care and status updates. The messages are sent in batches by each hospital's enterprise relationship management (ERM) system by using a VPN. The data sent from each hospital can have varying columns and formats.

Currently, a custom C# application is used to send the data to Health Interface. The application uses deprecated libraries and a new solution must be designed for this functionality.

Health Insights

ADatum has a web-based reporting system named Health Insights that shows hospital and patient insights to physicians and business users. The data is created from the data in Health Review and Health Interface, as well as manual entries.

Database Platform

Currently, the databases for all three applications are hosted on an out-of-date VMware cluster that has a single instance of Microsoft SQL Server 2012.

Problem Statements

ADatum identifies the following issues in its current environment:

- Over time, the data received by Health Interface from the hospitals has slowed, and the number of messages has increased. When a new hospital joins ADatum, Health Interface requires a schema modification due to the lack of data standardization. The speed of batch data processing is inconsistent.

Business Requirements Business Goals

ADatum identifies the following business goals:

- Migrate the applications to Azure whenever possible.
- Minimize the development effort required to perform data movement.
- Provide continuous integration and deployment for development, test, and production environments.
- Provide faster access to the applications and the data and provide more consistent application performance.
- Minimize the number of services required to perform data processing, development, scheduling, monitoring, and the operationalizing of pipelines.

Health Review Requirements

ADatum identifies the following requirements for the Health Review application:

- Ensure that sensitive health data is encrypted at rest and in transit.
- Tag all the sensitive health data in Health Review. The data will be used for auditing.

Health Interface Requirements

ADatum identifies the following requirements for the Health Interface application:

- Upgrade to a data storage solution that will provide flexible schemas and increased throughput for writing data. Data must be regionally located close to each hospital, and reads must display be the most recent committed version of an item.
- Reduce the amount of time it takes to add data from new hospitals to Health Interface. Support a more scalable batch processing solution in Azure.
- Reduce the amount of development effort to rewrite existing SQL queries.

Health Insights Requirements

ADatum identifies the following requirements for the Health Insights application:

- The analysis of events must be performed over time by using an organizational date dimension table.
- The data from Health Interface and Health Review must be available in Health Insights within 15 minutes of being committed.
- The new Health Insights application must be built on a massively parallel processing (MPP) architecture that will support the high performance of joins on large fact tables.

QUESTION 1

You need to recommend a security solution that meets the requirements of Health Review. What should you include in the recommendation?

A. dynamic data masking
B. Transport Layer Security (TLS)
C. Always Encrypted
D. row-level security

Correct Answer: C

Explanation/Reference:
Explanation:
Must ensure that sensitive health data is encrypted at rest and in transit.

Always Encrypted is a feature designed to protect sensitive data stored in Azure SQL Database or SQL Server databases. Always Encrypted allows clients to encrypt sensitive data inside client applications and never reveal the encryption keys to the database engine (SQL Database or SQL Server).

Reference:
https://docs.microsoft.com/en-us/azure/security/fundamentals/encryption-atrest
https://docs.microsoft.com/en-us/azure/security/fundamentals/database-security-overview

QUESTION 2
You need to recommend a solution to quickly identify all the columns in Health Review that contain sensitive health data. What should you include in the recommendation?

A. classifications
B. data masking
C. SQL Server auditing
D. Azure tags

Correct Answer: A

Explanation/Reference:
Explanation:
Data Discovery & Classification introduces a set of advanced capabilities aimed at protecting data and not just the data warehouse itself. Classification/Labeling – Sensitivity classification labels tagged on the columns can be persisted in the data warehouse itself.

Reference:
https://azure.microsoft.com/sv-se/blog/announcing-public-preview-of-data-discovery-classification-for-microsoft-azure-sql-data-warehouse/

Testlet 4 Overview

You are a data engineer for Trey Research. The company is close to completing a joint project with the government to build smart highways infrastructure across North America. This involves the placement of sensors and cameras to measure traffic flow, car speed, and vehicle details.

You have been asked to design a cloud solution that will meet the business and technical requirements of the smart highway.

Solution components Telemetry Capture

The telemetry capture system records each time a vehicle passes in front of a sensor. The sensors run on a custom embedded operating system and record the following telemetry data:

- Time
- Location in latitude and longitude
- Speed in kilometers per hour (kmph)
- Length of vehicle in meters

Visual Monitoring

The visual monitoring system is a network of approximately 1,000 cameras placed near highways that capture images of vehicle traffic every 2 seconds. The cameras record high resolution images. Each image is approximately 3 MB in size.

Requirements. Business

The company identifies the following business requirements:

- External vendors must be able to perform custom analysis of data using machine learning technologies.
- You must display a dashboard on the operations status page that displays the following metrics: telemetry, volume, and processing latency.
- Traffic data must be made available to the Government Planning Department for the purpose of modeling changes to the highway system.
- The traffic data will be used in conjunction with other data such as information about events such as sporting events, weather conditions, and population statistics. External data

used during the modeling is stored in on-premises SQL Server 2016 databases and CSV files stored in an Azure Data Lake Storage Gen2 storage account. Information about vehicles that have been detected as going over the speed limit during the last 30 minutes must be available to law enforcement officers.
Several law enforcement organizations may respond to speeding vehicles.

- The solution must allow for searches of vehicle images by license plate to support law enforcement investigations. Searches must be able to be performed using a query language and must support fuzzy searches to compensate for license plate detection errors.

Requirements. Security

The solution must meet the following security requirements:

- External vendors must not have direct access to sensor data or images.
- Images produced by the vehicle monitoring solution must be deleted after one month. You must minimize costs associated with deleting images from the data store.
- Unauthorized usage of data must be detected in real time. Unauthorized usage is determined by looking for unusual usage patterns.
- All changes to Azure resources used by the solution must be recorded and stored. Data must be provided to the security team for incident response purposes.

Requirements. Sensor data

You must write all telemetry data to the closest Azure region. The sensors used for the telemetry capture system have a small amount of memory available and so must write data as quickly as possible to avoid losing telemetry data.

QUESTION 1

You need to design the unauthorized data usage detection system. What Azure service should you include in the design?

A. Azure Analysis Services
B. Azure SQL Data Warehouse
C. Azure Databricks
D. Azure Data Factory

Correct Answer: B

Explanation/Reference:
Explanation:
SQL Database and SQL Data Warehouse
SQL threat detection identifies anomalous activities indicating unusual and potentially harmful attempts to access or exploit databases.

Advanced Threat Protection for Azure SQL Database and SQL Data Warehouse detects anomalous activities indicating unusual and potentially harmful attempts to access or exploit databases.

Scenario:
Requirements. Security
The solution must meet the following security requirements:
▪ Unauthorized usage of data must be detected in real time.
▪ Unauthorized usage is determined by looking for unusual usage patterns.

Reference:

https://docs.microsoft.com/en-us/azure/sql-database/sql-database-threat-detection-overview

Testlet 5 Case study

This is a case study. Case studies are not timed separately. You can use as much exam time as you would like to complete each case. However, there may be additional case studies and sections on this exam. You must manage your time to ensure that you are able to complete all questions included on this exam in the time provided.

To answer the questions included in a case study, you will need to reference information that is provided in the case study. Case studies might contain exhibits and other resources that provide more information about the scenario that is described in the case study. Each question is independent of the other questions in this case study.

At the end of this case study, a review screen will appear. This screen allows you to review your answers and to make changes before you move to the next section of the exam. After you begin a new section, you cannot return to this section.

To start the case study
To display the first question in this case study, click the **Next** button. Use the buttons in the left pane to explore the content of the case study before you answer the questions. Clicking these buttons displays information such as business requirements, existing environment, and problem statements. If the case study has an **All Information** tab, note that the information displayed is identical to the information displayed on the subsequent tabs. When you are ready to answer a question, click the **Question** button to return to the question.

Background

Trey Research is a technology innovator. The company partners with regional transportation department office to build solutions that improve traffic flow and safety. The company is developing the following solutions:

Solution	Comments
Real Time Response	This solution will detect sudden changes in traffic flow including slow downs and stops that persist for more than one minute. The system will automatically dispatch emergency response vehicles to investigate issues The solution will use a PySpark script to detect traffic flow changes. Script performance will be limited by available memory
Backtrack	This solution will allow public safety officials to locate vehicles on roadways that implement traffic sensors. The solution must report changes in real time.
Planning Assistance	Transportation organizations will use Planning Assistance to analyze traffic data. The solution will allow users to define reports based on queries of the traffic data. The reports can be used for the following analyses • current traffic load • correlation with recent local events susch as sporting events • historical traffic • tracking the travel of a single vehicle

Regional transportation departments installed traffic sensor systems on major highways across North America. Sensors record the following information each time a vehicle passes in front of a sensor:

- Time
- Location in latitude and longitude
- Speed in kilometers per second (kmps)
- License plate number
- Length of vehicle in meters

Sensors provide data by using the following structure:

```
{
   "time" : "2014-09-15T23:14:25.72511732",
    "location" : {
      "type": "Point",
      "coordinates": [
            31.9.
            -4.8
      ]
      },
   "speed": 66.2,
   "license_plate": "WA-AJ0072W",
   "vehicle_length": 4.5
}
```

Traffic sensors will occasionally capture an image of a vehicle for debugging purposes. You must optimize performance of saving/storing vehicle images.

Traffic sensor data

- Sensors must have permission only to add items to the SensorData collection.
- Traffic data insertion rate must be maximized.
- Once every three months all traffic sensor data must be analyzed to look for data patterns that indicate sensor malfunctions.
- Sensor data must be stored in a Cosmos DB named treydata in a collection named SensorData
- The impact of vehicle images on sensor data throughout must be minimized.

Backtrack

This solution reports on all data related to a specific vehicle license plate. The report must use data from the SensorData collection. Users must be able to filter vehicle data in the following ways:

- vehicles on a specific road
- vehicles driving above the speed limit

Planning Assistance

Data used for Planning Assistance must be stored in a sharded Azure SQL Database.

Data from the Sensor Data collection will automatically be loaded into the Planning Assistance database once a week by using Azure Data Factory. You must be able to manually trigger the data load process.

Privacy and security policy

- Azure Active Directory must be used for all services where it is available.
- For privacy reasons, license plate number information must not be accessible in Planning Assistance.
- Unauthorized usage of the Planning Assistance data must be detected as quickly as possible. Unauthorized usage is

determined by looking for an unusual pattern of usage.
- Data must only be stored for seven years.

Performance and availability

- The report for Backtrack must execute as quickly as possible.
- The SLA for Planning Assistance is 70 percent, and multiday outages are permitted. All data must be replicated to multiple geographic regions to prevent data loss.
- You must maximize the performance of the Real Time Response system.

Financial requirements

Azure resource costs must be minimized where possible.

Testlet 6 Case study

This is a case study. Case studies are not timed separately. You can use as much exam time as you would like to complete each case. However, there may be additional case studies and sections on this exam. You must manage your time to ensure that you are able to complete all questions included on this exam in the time provided.

To answer the questions included in a case study, you will need to reference information that is provided in the case study. Case studies might contain exhibits and other resources that provide more information about the scenario that is described in the case study. Each question is independent of the other questions in this case study.

At the end of this case study, a review screen will appear. This screen allows you to review your answers and to make changes before you move to the next section of the exam. After you begin a new section, you cannot return to this section.

To start the case study
To display the first question in this case study, click the **Next** button. Use the buttons in the left pane to explore the content of the case study before you answer the questions. Clicking these buttons displays information such as business requirements, existing environment, and problem statements. If the case study has an **All Information** tab, note that the information displayed is identical to the information displayed on the subsequent tabs. When you are ready to answer a question, click the **Question** button to return to the question.

Overview

You develop data engineering solutions for Graphics Design Institute, a global media company with offices in New York City, Manchester, Singapore, and Melbourne.

The New York office hosts SQL Server databases that stores massive amounts of customer data. The company also stores millions of images on a physical server located in the New York office. More than 2 TB of image data is added each day. The images are transferred from customer devices to the server in New York.

Many images have been placed on this server in an unorganized manner, making it difficult for editors to search images. Images should automatically have object and color tags generated. The tags must be stored in a document database, and be queried by SQL.

You are hired to design a solution that can store, transform, and visualize customer data.

Requirements Business

The company identifies the following business requirements:
- You must transfer all images and customer data to cloud storage and remove on-premises servers.
- You must develop an analytical processing solution for transforming customer data.
- You must develop an image object and color tagging solution.
- Capital expenditures must be minimized.
- Cloud resource costs must be minimized.

Technical

The solution has the following technical requirements:
- Tagging data must be uploaded to the cloud from the New York office location.
- Tagging data must be replicated to regions that are geographically close to company office locations.
- Image data must be stored in a single data store at minimum cost.
- Customer data must be analyzed using managed Spark clusters.
- Power BI must be used to visualize transformed customer data.
- All data must be backed up in case disaster recovery is required.

Security and optimization

All cloud data must be encrypted at rest and in transit. The solution must support:

- parallel processing of customer data
- hyper-scale storage of images
- global region data replication of processed image data

QUESTION 1
You plan to use Azure SQL Database to support a line of business app.

You need to identify sensitive data that is stored in the database and monitor access to the data. Which three actions should you recommend? Each correct answer presents part of the solution.

NOTE: Each correct selection is worth one point.

A. Enable Data Discovery and Classification.
B. Implement Transparent Data Encryption (TDE).
C. Enable Auditing.
D. Run Vulnerability Assessment.
E. Use Advanced Threat Protection.

Correct Answer: CDE

QUESTION 2

You have an Azure SQL database that has columns. The columns contain sensitive Personally Identifiable Information (PII) data.

You need to design a solution that tracks and stores all the queries executed against the PII data. You must be able to review the data in Azure Monitor, and the data must be available for at least 45 days.

Solution: You create a SELECT trigger on the table in SQL Database that writes the query to a new table in the database, and then executes a stored procedure that looks up the column classifications and joins to the query text.

Does this meet the goal?

A. Yes
B. No

Correct Answer: B

Explanation/Reference:
Explanation:
Instead add classifications to the columns that contain sensitive data and turn on Auditing.

Note: Auditing has been enhanced to log sensitivity classifications or labels of the actual data that were returned by the query. This would enable you to gain insights on who is accessing sensitive data.

Reference:
https://azure.microsoft.com/en-us/blog/announcing-public-preview-of-data-discovery-classification-for-microsoft-azure-sql-data-warehouse/

QUESTION 3

You are designing the security for an Azure SQL database.

You have an Azure Active Directory (Azure AD) group named Group1.

You need to recommend a solution to provide Group1 with read access to the database only. What should you include in the recommendation?

A. a contained database user
B. a SQL login
C. an RBAC role
D. a shared access signature (SAS)

Correct Answer: A

Explanation/Reference:
Explanation:
Create a User for a security group
A best practice for managing your database is to use Windows security groups to manage user access. That way you can simply manage the customer at the Security Group level in Active Directory granting appropriate permissions. To add a security group to SQL Data Warehouse, you use the Display Name of the security group as the principal in the CREATE USER statement.

CREATE USER [<Security Group Display Name>] FROM EXTERNAL PROVIDER WITH DEFAULT_SCHEMA = [<schema>];

In our AD instance, we have a security group called Sales Team with an alias of salesteam@company.com. To add this security group to SQL Data Warehouse you simply run the following statement:

CREATE USER [Sales Team] FROM EXTERNAL PROVIDER WITH DEFAULT_SCHEMA = [sales];

Reference:
https://blogs.msdn.microsoft.com/sqldw/2017/07/28/adding-ad-users-and-security-groups-to-azure-sql-data-warehouse/

QUESTION 4
You store data in a data warehouse in Azure Synapse
Analytics.

You need to design a solution to ensure that the data
warehouse and the most current data is available within one
hour of a datacenter failure. Which three actions should you
include in the design? Each correct answer presents part of the
solution.

NOTE: Each correct selection is worth one point.

A. Each day, restore the data warehouse from a geo-
   redundant backup to an available Azure region.
B. If a failure occurs, update the connection strings to point to
   the recovered data warehouse.
C. If a failure occurs, modify the Azure Firewall rules of the
   data warehouse.
D. Each day, create Azure Firewall rules that allow access to
   the restored data warehouse.
E. Each day, restore the data warehouse from a user-defined
   restore point to an available Azure region.

Correct Answer: BDE

Explanation/Reference:
Explanation:

E: You can create a user-defined restore point and restore from
the newly created restore point to a new data warehouse in a
different region. Note: A data warehouse snapshot creates a
restore point you can leverage to recover or copy your data
warehouse to a previous state.
A data warehouse restore is a new data warehouse that is
created from a restore point of an existing or deleted data
warehouse. On average within the same region, restore rates
typically take around 20 minutes.

Incorrect Answers:

A: SQL Data Warehouse performs a geo-backup once per day to a paired data center. The RPO for a geo-restore is 24 hours. You can restore the geo-backup to a server in any other region where SQL Data Warehouse is supported. A geo-backup ensures you can restore data warehouse in case you cannot access the restore points in your primary region.

Reference:
https://docs.microsoft.com/en-us/azure/sql-data-warehouse/backup-and-restore

QUESTION 5

You are designing a solution that will use Azure Databricks and Azure Data Lake Storage Gen2. From Databricks, you need to access Data Lake Storage directly by using a service principal. What should you include in the solution?

A. shared access signatures (SAS) in Data Lake Storage
B. access keys in Data Lake Storage
C. an organizational relationship in Azure Active Directory (Azure AD)
D. an application registration in Azure Active Directory (Azure AD)

Correct Answer: D

Explanation/Reference:
Explanation:
Create and grant permissions to service principal
If your selected the access method requires a service principal with adequate permissions, and you do not have one, follow these steps:

1. Create an Azure AD application and service principal that can access resources. Note the following properties:
    - client-id: An ID that uniquely identifies the application.
    - directory-id: An ID that uniquely identifies the Azure AD instance.
    - service-credential: A string that the application uses to prove its identity.

2. Register the service principal, granting the correct role assignment, such as Storage Blob Data

3. Contributor, on the Azure Data Lake Storage Gen2 account.

Reference:
https://docs.databricks.com/data/data-sources/azure/azure-datalake-gen2.html

www.ingramcontent.com/pod-product-compliance
Lightning Source LLC
Chambersburg PA
CBHW071253050326
40690CB00011B/2374